More praise for *Working Class Rage*

"Few have worked more diligently and thoughtfully than Tex Sample in understanding what counts in working-class communities and why the pain and outrage felt by working men and women have mounted in recent years. In *Working Class Rage*, Sample not only documents why that outrage is in order, but he offers a basis in Christian ethics for focusing it on ways to build a more just and equitable society."
—**Neal F. Fisher**, President Emeritus, Garrett-Evangelical Theological Seminary, Evanston, IL

"Sample cuts to the core in *Working Class Rage*. Straight-talking and deep-diving, he analyzes political history, social studies of the working class, and stories of individuals and communities, all with his sharp mind and zingy humor. He uncovers the complicated realities of working-class life and the systems that oppress working people. Further, he points to the failings of virtually everyone and every system in the US. Both the people (us) and our leaders have repeatedly made social, political, and economic choices that ignore the lives and hardships of people in the working class, favoring instead the wealthy and elite. Drawing from biblical and theological reflection, Sample proposes a way forward—a vision of the common good, embodied in very practical action. Thank you, Tex!"
—**Mary Elizabeth Moore**, Dean and professor of theology and education, Boston University School of Theology, Boston, MA

"Reading *Working Class Rage*, I feel I'm in the presence of a fearless bearer of news from the real world—news about the dynamics and abuse of power, the persistence of prejudice, and the resilience of gospel solutions. Plainspoken and passionate, Tex Sample speaks where many of us are unaccountably silent. Across race and class, Tex is doing drastically important work, the work of public theology."
—**Ray Waddle**, author, *Undistorted God* and *Against the Grain*; editor, *Reflections* magazine, Yale Divinity School, New Haven, CT

Other Abingdon Press books by Tex Sample

A Christian Justice for the Common Good
Earthy Mysticism: Spirituality for Unspiritual People
Blue Collar Resistance and the Politics of Jesus
White Soul: Country Music, the Church, and Working Americans
Hard Living People & Mainstream Christians

TEX SAMPLE

WORKING CLASS RAGE

A FIELD GUIDE TO WHITE ANGER AND PAIN

Abingdon Press™
Nashville

**WORKING CLASS RAGE:
A FIELD GUIDE TO WHITE ANGER AND PAIN**

Copyright © 2018 by Abingdon Press

All rights reserved

Library of Congress Cataloging-in-Publication data has been requested.

ISBN 978-1-5018-6813-9

All scripture quotations unless noted otherwise are taken from the Common English Bible. Copyright © 2011 by the Common English Bible. All rights reserved. Used by permission. www.CommonEnglishBible.com.

Scripture quotations marked NRSV are taken from The New Revised Standard Version of the Bible, copyright 1989, Division of Christian Education of the National Council of the Churches of Christ in the United States of America. Used by permission. All rights reserved.

18 19 20 21 22 23 24 25 26 27—10 9 8 7 6 5 4 3 2 1
MANUFACTURED IN THE UNITED STATES OF AMERICA

Dedicated to

Jeep Pickett, Gang Pusher

Bernell Birch

Snooks Britt

John Case

Ronnie Smith

These men are the gang I worked with in the oil field for four summers that enabled me to go to college. They apprenticed me and kept me safe. Bennie London was the field supervisor and gave me the job I really needed.

CONTENTS

PREFACE

In the summer of 2017 David Teel at Abingdon Press called and asked if I would be interested in writing a book on the white working class. Since I had been studying and writing on that subject for years, it piqued my interest, especially so because I had been examining growing inequalities in our country, which were generating a deep and pervasive anger. So, I asked David if I could do the book on white working-class rage. He seemed to like the idea, and this book is the result.

Chapter 1 provides a brief overview of this context of white working-class rage, especially the growing rule by corporate America and the rich, a glut of incentives and subsidies going to the top corporations and their scions with the consequent growing inequalities of income and wealth.

Chapter 2 begins an attempt to identify who is the white working class, turning first to statistical and polling data. While these are helpful, they are not enough. Chapters 3 and 4 report on significant ethnographic studies of white working-class people in urban and rural America, respectively, in an attempt not so much to define as to describe the flesh and blood realities of white working people.

Chapter 5 addresses the issue of racism in both its prejudicial and systemic and structural forms, especially in its established institutions and agents, in order to challenge the scapegoating of the white working class on this issue but also to diagnose more carefully its white working-class expressions, in order to be able to take more effective action.

The next chapter moves to the indigenous practices of white working-class people so that we know how to seek the common good, not just more effectively, but also with more respect for their idioms and practices. As important as this indigenous work is, however, grassroots, down on the ground, community action is necessary; so chapter 7 reports work being done in cities, counties, and states in urban and rural America by means of coalition strategies involving white working-class people.

The last chapter provides a biblical and theological rationale by which, on the one hand, to critique white working-class commitments; but, on the other hand, to affirm central dimensions of their culture that open doors economically, politically, and spiritually for more faithful and vital life.

About me: I do not come at these issues from a remote, abstract position. My father spent most of his life in working-class jobs. My mother worked more than twenty years in a nonunion factory making the minimum wage. In my extended family today my daughter is a hairdresser, and my son has been a working-class man until the last two years and now owns and operates a karate dojo and martial arts store. His wife works in human relations and is a native of Mexico and a naturalized US citizen. Two of my granddaughters are Japanese American, one a bartender and the other a firefighter. The other granddaughter is developmentally disabled and receives Medicaid. My grandson is a Teamster, and his spouse is a factory worker in a Harley-Davidson plant that will relocate in a year's time. My wife is a musician and an artist, and I am a professor emeritus of a theological school, but we live at the edge of this working-class world every day.

I am grateful to the community organizations with which I am active in Kansas City: the Faith and Labor Alliance, the Human Dignity and Economic Justice Coalition, Jobs with Justice, Stand Up KC, the Metro Organization for Racial and Economic Equity, and Urban Summit. My wife Peggy and I are active in the multiracial Grand Avenue Temple United Methodist Church, where a majority of the congregation is poor and a large plurality is homeless.

I am indebted to those who read part or all of the manuscript and commented on it: Judy Ancel, Tom Bandy, Bishop Ken Carder, Congressman Emanuel Cleaver II, Cheryll Doughty, Michael Enriquez, Brian Grimm,

Khadijah Hardaway, Libby Manning, Derek Nelson, Robert Sartin, Max Skidmore, Bishop James Tindall, and Ray Waddle. I have been blessed by the editing of David Teel. Working with him is a gift of the first order. To Sam Mann, I am especially grateful. During the seven months I worked on this book, he talked with me several times each week and read no few pages more than once. I am, of course, responsible for what remains.

As I worked on the manuscript I had opportunity to lecture on its contents to the Great Plains and Oklahoma United Methodist retired clergy; the All Souls Unitarian Universalist Church in Kansas City; the Church Women's Legislative Conference in Topeka, Kansas; the Wabash Pastoral Institute; and the North Carolina United Methodist Annual Conference "Crossroads Retreat: Prophetic Living in a Broken World." I am grateful for their hospitality and the opportunity to work on this material with them.

Finally, Jesus said that we are neither given nor taken in marriage in the reign of God. I have asked for a special dispensation because one lifetime is not enough to be wedded to Peggy Sample.

THE CONTEXT OF WHITE WORKING-CLASS RAGE

When I saw the ad for J. D. Vance's *Hillbilly Elegy*, I ordered it immediately, anticipating that I would "be acquainted" with its people. Indeed, I was. While my hometown was not Appalachia, I knew many poor people and dealt with a wide variety of people growing up. My father was the owner and operator of the 13 Taxi Company in Brookhaven, Mississippi, and at twelve years of age I started answering the phone there. At sixteen I got a commercial license so I could drive one of the four cabs. Added to my upbringing were two of my uncles and one aunt who were actively engaged in the bootleg business. So, I was acquainted with the poor, with working people, and the underbelly of our community.

Vance's poignant story is a riveting one of his growing up initially in Appalachian Kentucky, but mostly in the Rust Belt town of Middletown in southwest Ohio. With a drug-dependent mother, he is "saved" from that situation by a grandfather, and especially a grandmother, who were central to his making it eventually to the Marines, Ohio State University, and Yale Law School. The book is a gripping page-turner; nevertheless, I grew restive as I read along. His mother's tragic drug dependency was a story I had heard many times. But the more I read *Hillbilly Elegy*, the more convinced I was that Vance did not know the difference between his mother's addictive pathology and the larger culture of Appalachian life. His comments about people gaming the welfare system, for example, gave anecdotal "evidence" of a problem that is not nearly so much related to the culture as to the economic devastation of the hillbilly lives he claims to represent.

Toward the end of the book I realized what was going on. Acknowledging his conservative position Vance does what conservatives tend to do. According to him, the basic problems of his hillbillies are those of culture, not class. It is the old right-wing ploy of reducing the ravages of economics and class—and, in other discussions, race—to the inadequacies of culture. At one point Vance says that "public policy can help, but there is no government that can fix these problems for us."[1] He states further, "These problems were not created by government or corporations or anyone else. We created them, and only we [his people] can fix them."[2] He insists that we "stop blaming Obama or Bush or faceless companies and ask ourselves what we can do to make things better."[3]

Vance's book is virtually oblivious to the history and economics of Appalachia and southwestern Ohio. He does not give an account, for example, of the "pillage and plunder" of Appalachia by coal and timber companies. The dominance of coal brought work camps with low wages and company stores with hiked-up prices. In Southern Appalachia the timber barons brought clear-cutting practices of the forests "and left environmental and economic devastation in their wake."[4] In the process the coal and timber industries converted "independent farmers and craftspeople into laborers treated like nothing more than replaceable parts."[4] Meanwhile, many were exiled to the North in a huge diaspora.

The great contradiction of Vance's book is that he is now ensconced in a venture capitalist firm in San Francisco and is telling his "hillbillies" that they have to be responsible for their own lives and work out their problems basically without help from the policies and actions of the state.

---

1. J. D. Vance, *Hillbilly Elegy* (New York: HarperCollins, 2016), 194, 255–56. For his "analysis" of Middletown see 255.

2. Ibid., 256.

3. Ibid.

4. Ibid.

All of this in a financial capitalism that is sucking on every government tit it can find. I suppose, however, that this is quite fitting for his stated possible plans for a political career as a Republican or, for that matter, a neoliberal Democrat.

Vance's book participates in a wider litany of public commentary that tends to blame the white working class for their current condition. In America today we find stigmatizing, stereotyping, the use of racial epithets, and, yes, romantic and nostalgic characterizations of this important group of Americans. The basic attempt here is to get in touch with the lives of white working-class people primarily through down on the ground studies of them, which will be examined in chapters 3 and 4.

Before turning to studies of white working-class Americans, however, we need to address the context confronted by them. What has been going on? What is the source of their fear, their pain, and their anger? How are we to understand their rage? I demonstrate in this chapter that white working people have endured very hard times and great social, political, and economic reversals over the last forty-five years. They have painful reasons to be afraid and furious.

Neoliberalism and the Abandonment of the Working Class

From the end of World War II until the mid-1970s the United States political economy basically followed the New Deal that originated under the administration of President Franklin Delano Roosevelt. This period of time was known as "the great compromise." This compromise lay in the fact that American labor, at least great numbers of workers, made good money with benefits and pensions. These payoffs, however, often required jobs that were routine, repetitive, and monotonous.

In the mid-1970s this began to change. Vietnam War protests, the civil rights movement, exposés of big business such as that of auto safety by Ralph Nader, and the baby boomer counterculture scared key elements in big business. In response a massive, extremist right-wing reaction began, which would take over the previous Eisenhower form of the Republican

Party and eventually make major gains in the Democratic Party during the administrations of presidents Jimmy Carter, Bill Clinton, and Barack Obama.

I call this movement the *neoliberal turn.* The term itself has had various usages across its history, but here I work with it in a very specific way to characterize what has happened in recent decades in the United States. Neoliberalism is a reaction against mixed-market economic policies and a return to "free market" capitalism as envisioned by right-wing adherents. It combats government regulation, seeks to lower wages and taxes, opposes welfare spending, and actively works to weaken unions and labor organizing. Committed to privatization and fiscal austerity, it fights to give the private sector the dominant role in the economy.

Neoliberalism began with a powerful right-wing attack initiated in the mid-1970s. Its impact on the working class—on whites and people of color—has been devastating, as we shall see.

The Right-Wing Assault on America

In 1971 Louis F. Powell Jr. was invited by the US Chamber of Commerce to draft a confidential memorandum entitled "Attack on the American Free Enterprise System." Powell, a veteran of World War II, and a key attorney for the Tobacco Institute, wrote in his memo that the free enterprise system was under attack and in desperate difficulty.

His memorandum was a call for corporate America to take a more aggressive role in shaping US public opinion to address an ideological crisis. American culture had to be turned around, political discourse had to move in new directions, and public opinion had to be changed and won over. Joined by conservatives like Irving Kristol and William Simon, they built "a right-wing ideology machine" that over the next four decades became "an imposing network of corporate sponsors, business groups, think tanks, media watchdog organizations, radio and television talk shows, Internet sites, conservative intellectuals, and right-wing politicians."[5]

---

5. Edward Royce, *Poverty & Power: The Problem of Structural Inequality* (New York: Rowman and Littlefield, 2009), 173. Royce provides a brief, well-documented history of the politics, corporations, and media of the right wing over the past nearly five decades.

Rich donors provided huge amounts of money to support this right-wing push, funding for which came from wealthy conservative family foundations like the Bradley Foundation, the Smith Richardson Foundation, the Scaife Family Foundation, the Castle Rock Foundation (the Coors family), the Koch family foundations, and the John M. Olin Foundation.[6]

Existing conservative think tanks such as the American Enterprise Institute (1943), the Hoover Foundation (1919), and the Hudson Institute (1961) took on new life and growth during the 70s, soon to be joined by the Heritage Foundation (1973), the Cato Institute (1978), and the Manhattan Institute (1978). One report estimates that right-wing think tanks spent $1 billion advancing the conservative cause in the 1990s alone. "Conservative think tanks and corporate foundations—this combination of 'brains and money'—gave the right in the 1980s and 1990s the institutional standing and financial wherewithal to dominate political debate in the United States."[7]

Sharply concerned as well by what they saw as media bias that was unfriendly to business, the right began a twofold strategy: a program of intimidation from the outside and taking control on the inside. The first strategy began with watchdog organizations monitoring media to detect and publicize any bias they believed they detected and to push news programs to offer conservative points of view. With right-wing politicians and commentators joining this strategy they became very successful, especially with charges of "liberal bias." Royce comments that the "din" of conservative voices drowned out the left, while mainstream media overcompensated in their attempts to be neutral.[8]

These pundits appeared frequently on radio, TV, Internet sites, syndicated columns, and right-wing newspapers and journals. Others, like Bill O'Reilly (until recently), Sean Hannity, and Rush Limbaugh had their own television and radio shows.

---

6. Ibid.

7. Ibid.

8. Ibid., 174.

At the same time, conservative corporate leaders took aggressive steps to alter political and economic power in the larger society through corporate mergers, widespread efforts of deregulation, and anti-union campaigns. By campaign funding of conservative politicians in the Congress, state legislators, governors' offices, and many local governments, these right-wing forces changed the political and economic landscape of America. Meanwhile, Fox Fictional News (my title) and people like Rush Limbaugh and Sean Hannity served as mouthpieces for right-wing propaganda.

All of this encouraged large donations from conservative foundations to right-wing think tanks and the spurring of a powerful current of ideas, intellectuals, pundits, and organizations. Beginning in the 70s and 80s the conservative movement became the dominant influence in political life in America.

The conservative movement was well under way by the time of Ronald Reagan's election to the US presidency and his fiction that a rising tide in the economy lifts all boats. What we have discovered since is that Reagan's rising tide actually made more room for yachts, as we see in the increases in inequality of income and wealth below. Further, his argument that the problem of government *is* government itself diverted the attention of many away from significant problems with "trickle-down economics," which George H.W. Bush called rightly "voodoo economics." Both of these claims about government and a rising tide were powerful cheers led by Reagan, the most effective cheerleader of the right. These comments, in effect, functioned as a subterfuge to remove protections of the American people from the excesses of a rapacious capitalism and, in fact, furthered the role of government as servant to the rich and corporate America. There are, to be sure, many problems with government but clearly not the ones Reagan identified. He lived in a B-movie world and acted out a soap opera drama filled with fictional plots that made legal thieves of the real robbers of the American Dream.

The rise of neoliberalism also led to greater political activity on the part of the US Chamber of Commerce, so that today the Chamber is a major right-wing force and a lobbying machine. While the Chamber is the eight-hundred-pound gorilla stomping through the Washington jungle, a host of other smaller but predatory animals are on the prowl. Why? Because it pays off corporate greed.[9]

The Complicity of the Democratic Party and Its Presidents

It would be a mistake, however, to blame the entirety of the outcomes visited upon working Americans on the right-wing movement alone. By their complicity, the Democratic Party and its presidents for the last forty-five years are guilty of abandoning working people in this country. If anything, they deserve more of the shame because, at least since the time of Franklin Roosevelt and his New Deal, the Democrats were supposed to be the party of the people, especially working people. I will not go into detail about the Democratic Party but simply in this space lay out the failures of Democratic presidents, which in most cases reflect that party's accommodation of the right-wing movement in the United States.

I begin with President Jimmy Carter, who first broke with the New Deal tradition. It was he who cut out public works projects, rejected organized labor, and with a Democratic Congress enacted the first actually sizable tax cuts for the rich. Moreover, he enacted the first of the big deregulations, and with Paul Volcker, put the country on an austerity program with highly negative impacts on workaday Americans.[10]

But Carter was a piker compared to Bill Clinton. Not only did Clinton collude with Newt Gingrich but on occasion worked against his own party in Congress to pass his so-called neoliberal programs. The "welfare reform" he enacted in coalition with Newt Gingrich continued Ronald Reagan's assault on the poor, and Clinton's successful endorsement of NAFTA and his trade agreements with China served corporate America at considerable cost to working people in this country. He, too, lowered

---

9. Ibid., 173.

10. I am dependent in this section on Thomas Frank's *Listen Liberal; or, Whatever Happened to the Party of the People* (New York: Metropolitan Books, 2016). It is a searing indictment of the Democratic Party and its presidents. Frank's discussion of Carter is on pages 53–55, 57.

taxes on the rich and corporate America and was a servant to Wall Street to the detriment of the greater American public.

Instrumental in eliminating the Glass-Steagall Act, Clinton's legislative work, along with the inanities of George W. Bush, led directly to the 2008 collapse of the economy. Deregulation, eliminating protections of the people from the excesses of Wall Street and corporate America, were big on the Clinton list of actions. These included derivatives, the telecom industry, electricity, and interstate banking. And, of course, he was key to the passage of a capital gains tax. The Clinton administration also played a pivotal role in another "reform," this time of criminal justice, which led to the massive incarnation of people of color now so prominent in our country.[11]

Moving on to the presidency of Barack Obama is painful for me. I had great hopes for him and his leadership of the country. And, like Clinton, he did some good things (e.g., the Affordable Care Act, with some qualifications), but Thomas Frank captures very well the work of his administration when he says Obama "repeatedly sacrificed working people's interests because it conflicted with the interests of the upper strata."[12] For example, he managed to get through Congress a large stimulus package at a critical time, but the major "part of it was wasted on tax cuts designed to lure Republican votes." It also called for "shovel ready" projects, but what it did not do was develop federal job creation because such job programs would have increased the federal workforce. So, instead, Obama's so-called *New* New Deal doled the money out to others; and while unemployment did finally come down, wages remained stagnant, convincing the president, says Frank, that there was nothing that could really be done for working people.[13]

A well-publicized failure was a Democratic proposal that would have permitted adjustments in mortgages for homeowners who came before bankruptcy judges. Called *cramdown*, this proposal would've been of

---

11. Ibid. See Frank's discussion of the actions of Bill Clinton's administration on pages 81–105. Yes, it is true that unemployment went down and the budget was balanced, making Clinton a miracle for some, until the dot-com bubble burst in 2000.

12. Ibid., 147.

13. Ibid., 146.

extraordinary assistance to millions of homeowners, albeit not helpful to mortgage holders. When the proposal came before the Senate, Obama did nothing, and bank lobbyists defeated it readily.

In addition, the Employee Free Choice Act would have facilitated collective bargaining between workers and management and could have helped reverse the long-term decline of the percentage of union membership in the workforce. Obama endorsed this measure initially, but he withdrew his support under pressure from Walmart and Chamber of Commerce lobbyists. Among these lobbyists were former assistants to John Kerry, Rahm Emanuel, some Democratic senators, and the secretary of labor.

A good many other things, such as Obama's support of the Trans-Pacific Partnership (TPP) trade agreement, served the interests of Big Pharma and Silicon Valley, for example, but had no protections for American workers. Finally, and damning, Obama ignored criminal behavior by banks and other financial institutions that led to the 2008 economic crisis. Some say there was nothing he could do in the last six years of his presidency because of the intransigence of Republicans in Congress. Yet the office of the president has executive powers regarding antitrust laws that were clearly at Obama's command. The timing was perfect; antitrust actions would have been powerfully popular, but Obama did nothing. As Thomas Frank reports, "Anti-monopoly investigations conducted by Obama's Justice Department went from a barely breathing four in 2009 to a flat zero in 2014."[14]

Clearly our country has been in the grips of a neoliberalism that for more than four decades has waged war against working people, both white and people of color. We now take a look at some of the consequences of this neoliberal turn.

Productivity and Wages

We begin by looking at the fact that working people have continued to produce in this country, but their wages have not by any means kept

---

14. Ibid., 156.

pace with their production. This "decoupling of pay and productivity" has occurred in the United States over recent decades in sharp contrast to the twenty-five-year period following World War II. From 1943 until the mid-1970s productivity rose more than 103 percent, as did wages. However, since that time the hourly compensation of the great mass of American workers has not risen with productivity. The Economic Policy Institute reports that while net productivity rose 72.2 percent between 1973 and 2014, "inflation adjusted hourly compensation of the median worker rose just 8.7% or 0.20% annually..., with essentially all of this growth occurring between 1995 and 2002." Moreover, the EPI found that "real hourly compensation of production, nonsupervisory workers, who make up 80% of the workforce, also shows pay stagnation for most of the period since 1973." Further, since 2000, "the gap between productivity and pay has risen even faster." Finally, Thomas Frank, brought to national attention by his book, *What's Wrong with Kansas,* reports that from 1930 to 1980 the bottom 90 percent[15] of the population took home 70 percent of the gross income gains, but from 1980 to the present the bottom 90 percent of the population pocketed none of this growth.[16] No wonder working people are mad as hell.

Of course, globalization has affected relationships between productivity and wages and between income growth and its shares, but why have these shifts fallen so heavily and systematically on the bottom half to 60 percent of the American people? I suggest that globalization is too abstract of a term; what we have had is *neoliberal* globalization, a very different matter. What these data on productivity and wages demonstrate is the increasing loss of power of working people in the US and the peripheralization of their lives to the edges of decision-making and social policy, a dynamic affecting the wider public in this country, as we shall see next.

---

15.   Josh Bivens and Lawrence Mishel, "Understanding the Historic Divergence between Productivity and a Typical Worker's Pay," Economic Policy Institute, September 2, 2015, http://www.epi.org/publication/understanding-the-historic-divergence-between-produc tivity-and-a-typical-workers-pay-why-it-matters-and-why-its-real/. With a net productivity growth rate of 21.6 percent, compensation for the median worker grew just 1.8 percent.

16.   Thomas Frank, public lecture at the Kansas City Public Library, April 6, 2017.

Government of Elites, by Elites, and for Elites

Martin Gilens and Benjamin Page studied the outcomes of a total of 1,779 policy issues.[17] Their results show that the preferences of the average American had "a minuscule, near zero, statistically non-significant impact upon public policy."[18] Further, they found a negative relationship between the alignments of "the most influential, business-oriented groups" and the wishes of the average citizen, and that the wants of economic elites have far more singular influence on policy change than do the preferences of average citizens.[19] When the preferences of average citizens are met, it is because their views coincide with those of business elites "who wield the actual influence."[20]

The work of Gilens and Page is a devastating challenge to the idea that America is a government of the people, by the people, and for the people. It is rather a government of elites, by elites, and for elites. This alone should be enough to enrage the great majority of Americans; it certainly feeds into the rage of the white working class. If this were not bad enough, the amount of welfare provided for corporate America and its wealthy few should gall us even more. I call it *wealth*fare, a basic component of neoliberalism.

*Wealth*fare

In his 1976 run for the Republican presidential nomination, and again in his 1980 run for the presidency, Ronald Reagan frequently used the term *welfare queen* at campaign events. Depicting these women as parasites on the larger public, he portrayed them as depleting public resources

---

17. Martin Gilens and Benjamin I. Page, "Testing Theories of American Politics: Elites, Interest Groups, and Average Citizens," *Perspectives on Politics* 12, no. 3 (September 2014): 564–81, accessed December 8, 2017, https://scholar.princeton.edu/sites/default/files/mgilens /files/gilens_and_page_2014_-testing_theories_of_american_politics.doc.pdf.

18. Ibid., 575.

19. Ibid., 576.

20. Ibid.

while living out destructive behavior. Subsequent studies of social welfare abuse, however, found that only a small percentage of recipients worked the system illegally. The demeaning use of the term *welfare queen* was for the sake of politically manipulating the public; and the stereotyping of welfare recipients became an influential, ideological tool to erode public support for Aid to Families with Dependent Children and redistributive policies in general.

Our brave politicians come down severely on so-called welfare queens, but their leniency toward *wealthfare kings* in corporate America, and among the rich, is an example of towering immorality. To spell out only a small sliver of this *wealthfare*, I turn first to the work of Pulitzer Prize–winning investigative reporter David Cay Johnston.

In his book, *Free Lunch*, Johnston demonstrates with great force that in America we are "creating a society of corporate socialism at the top and raw market forces down below."[21] Johnston describes a host of situations in which corporations and the rich take from the many in order to line the pockets of the top tenth of one percent. For example, he reports $100 million that went to Warren Buffett and $1.3 billion that went to the New York Yankees and the New York Mets. Time and again he describes how the super-rich rely on public handouts and wasteful entitlements. In Johnston's tour de force of public criticism he belies the myth that those who are dependent on public largesse come mainly from the bottom rungs of the society. Johnston takes on hedge fund tax breaks, corporate subsidies, Wall Street lobbyists, and the hustling of our healthcare system, among others, and sets in sharp relief the outrageous distance between the rich and the rest of us.

In this space I can report just one illustration of the federal government's largesse to corporate America; that is, Sam Walton's Walmart stores. In getting his start Walton made "use of free land, long-term leases at below-market rates, pocketing sales taxes, even getting workers trained at government expense" to take as much advantage of corporate welfare as he could. Johnston reports that Walton had a particular attraction for "government-sponsored industrial revenue bonds." These bonds made it

---

21. David Cay Johnston, *Free Lunch: How the Wealthiest Americans Enrich Themselves at Government Expense and Stick You with the Bill* (New York: Penguin Books, 2007), 293.

possible for him to pay less interest than he would have had he used corporate bonds through the market economy.[22]

When Walton first started using subsidies to finance Walmart, no one paid much attention so that official records and media reports are negligible. This means that "the full scope of its [Walmart's] taking [of subsidies] probably will never be known."[23] However, Phil Mattera of Good Jobs First, a group supported almost completely by foundations that investigate corporate subsidies, examined old securities documents and news reports to determine how much *wealthfare* (my term) Walmart had received. Mattera and his associates discovered "proof of subsidies at just 91 of more than 4,000 Walmart stores" and mainly related to those built recently.[24] In addition, the Mattera team found subsidies at eighty-four of ninety-one distribution centers. "The subsidies Mattera could pin down totaled $1 billion and change." But such a figure is far less than what Walmart actually received. Johnston reports that B. John Bisio, a Walmart spokesperson, told the *Telegraph Herald* newspaper in Dubuque, Iowa, that "it is common" for Walmart to go after subsidies for new stores and receives them in about one-third of all projects."[25] This would mean Walmart got fourteen times more subsidies than Mattera and his team found.

Johnston's expose was published in 2007, right before the Wall Street infractions that brought about the Great Recession. So, let's jump ahead almost ten years to the results of a more recent study. Oxfam America, a global movement of people working together to end the injustice of poverty, published a study in 2014 and updated it in 2017. They report that from 2008 to 2014 the fifty largest companies they studied

- got back $27 "in federal loans, loan guarantees and bailouts" for each dollar paid in taxes;

- spent $2.6 billion on lobbying to get back almost $11.2 trillion in federal loans, loan guarantees, and bailouts;

22. Ibid., 99.

23. Ibid., 100.

24. Ibid., 100-101.

25. Ibid., quoted by Johnston, 100.

- used lobbying to provide an extraordinary "return on investment" of $130 in tax breaks and more than $4,000 in federal loans, loan guarantees and bailouts for every dollar spent on lobbying as a group;

- made nearly $4 trillion in profits around the world during these same years, and made lucrative use of offshore tax shelters to pay a tax rate of only 26.5 percent—significantly less than the statutory rate of 35 percent and less than that paid in other developed nations; in fact, only five of the fifty corporations paid the statutory rate; and

- utilized "an opaque and secretive network of more than 1,600 disclosed subsidiaries in tax havens to stash about $1.4 trillion offshore." However, these numbers do not reveal thousands of further subsidiaries that remain unknown because of "weak reporting requirements" to the Securities and Exchange Commission.[26]

But there is more. American multinationals moved $700 billion from the nations where their profits were actually made to other places with either no tax rates or very low ones.[27] This led to a major shift in tax burdens. Note that in 1952 corporations paid one-third of the federal budget. Now they provide just nine percent, a figure that will be reduced even further with the so-called tax reform enacted by Trump and a Republican-dominated Congress in 2018.

The Oxfam study observes that when corporate America finds ways to avoid taxes, the government revenues required fall on small businesses and working people. Their analysis finds that each taxpayer would have to pay $1,026 in taxes annually to compensate for this tax dodging by corporations and wealthy persons. So, that tax dodging, tax haven abuse, use of offshore financial centers, loopholes in federal tax legislation, shifting ownership assets to paper-tiger subsidiaries in other locations, and renouncing US citizenship through the purchase of a foreign subsidiary in a jurisdiction with low taxes: these are only some of the practices of a massive scale of tax avoidance by corporate America.[28]

---

26. "Broken at the Top," Oxfam Media Briefing, Oxfam America, April 14, 2016, https://www.oxfamamerica.org/static/media/files/Broken_at_the_Top_4.14.2016.pdf.

27. Ibid.

28. Ibid.

Inequality in Income and Wealth

As one might expect, the relationship of productivity to wages, the impact of business interests on our governing policies, and the indefensible *wealthfare* for corporate America and the rich have contributed massively to the growing inequalities of income and wealth in the United States. Let us look first at the grotesque disparities of income. The 10 percent at the top of America's income pyramid now average almost nine times the income of the bottom 90 percent. When one reaches the heights of US income, the top 1 percent has thirty-eight times that of the bottom 90 percent, and the top 0.1 percent takes in more than 184 times what the bottom 90 percent receives.

The disparities of wealth are far greater than those of income. Of the $67 trillion of US family wealth in 2013, 76 percent of that wealth belonged to the top 10 percent. Even so, there were significant differences among the top 10 percent. To get into the top 10 percent, you needed at least $942,000, but the average of this group in wealth was $4 million. If you were in the remaining top half—averaging $316,000 per family—you represented some 23 percent of the total US wealth.

In contrast, the bottom half of the US population receives only 1 percent of the total. Those in the 26th to 50th percentiles averaged just $36,000 in total family wealth, an amount that would buy a new mid-range automobile. Meanwhile, the bottom quarter of the population had negative wealth; that is, they owed an average of $13,000 per family.[29]

The American Dream

One should not be surprised that flat wages and growing inequalities of wealth have a significant impact on the American Dream. Recent research by Raj Chetty and associates at Stanford University provides compelling evidence for the growing lack of confidence in the American Dream. Gaining access to millions of individual tax records across

---

29. All of these data come from the Congressional Budget Office as reported in Jeanne Sahadi, "The Richest 10% Hold 76% of the Wealth," CNN Money, August 18, 2016, http://money.cnn.com/2016/08/18/pf/wealth-inequality/index.html.

decades, they sought to determine the likelihood that people born at different times would make more money than their parents had. They discovered that babies born in 1940 had a 92 percent chance of making a better household income than their parents. From that point on, however, the probability began to decrease, so that those born in 1950 had a 79 percent possibility; in 1960, 62 percent; in 1970, 61 percent; and in 1980, 50 percent.[30]

To summarize and conclude, no investigation of the white working class can ignore these massive dynamics now occurring in the political economy of the United States: the rise of a powerful neoliberalism and its promotion of the greed of a rapacious capitalism; the growing disparity of productivity and wages; the domination of political processes by corporate America and its wealthy scions; the massive hypocrisy of highly subsidized big business addicted to wealthfare; and the progressive diminishment of the American Dream. This is the context of white working-class rage.

These pervasive dynamics impact the white working class even when the culprits are not adequately named. These dynamics include: not having a living wage, or having one but being insecure about what tomorrow portends; worrying about your children's future, knowing deep in your bones that the rich rule and that the political system is fixed; knowing that this country is not responsive to you; and, yes, too often blaming *down* and identifying *up*, condemning the poor and playing the lottery; and, hating the unending struggle and wishing you were rich. These are among the things of a free-floating rage, sometimes misdirected and too often leading to social and political withdrawal; sometimes caught up in racist and anti-immigrant expressions; and, at other times worshipping the idols of nation and militaristic expanse, captive to American exceptionalism and Manifest Destiny and, in spite of all, hooked on the American Dream, sort of.

---

30. The work of Chetty and associates is reported by David Leonhardt, "The American Dream, Quantified at Last," Sunday Review, *New York Times*, December 8, 2016, https://www.nytimes.com/2016/12/08/opinion/the-american-dream-quantified-at-last.html. See also the Chetty, et al article, "The Fading American Dream: Trends in Absolute Income Mobility since 1940" *Science*, April 24, 2017, science.sciencemag.org/content/early/2017/04/21/science.aal4617.full.

But the people of the white working class are a complicated people. The great majority of them bust their tails working at hard jobs that rack their bodies and don't pay enough. They support their families and draw dignity and identity from protecting and taking care of the people they love. When war comes, they are among the first to enlist and among the first to die. In all the twists and turns of the crazy history of this country they endure. Barring the global devastation of a nuclear war or some absolute ecological disaster, when capitalism is dead and America is no more, working people will continue to labor in the economies and political rule of worlds yet to come. They abide.

Perhaps this alone is reason enough to try to understand who they are in this day and time, develop an appreciation for the complexity of their lives, and shape among those of us in different stations a sensibility of such sufficient grasp as to appreciate who they are. We turn there in the next chapter.

CHAPTER 2

WHO IS THE WHITE WORKING CLASS?

Who are the white working-class people in the United States? What do they believe? How do they think? What do they value? To whom do they relate, and why? Some say that under their hard hats, service worker caps, and exaggerated hairdos lies a desolate and abject domain. My liberal and progressive friends and colleagues often call them "rednecks," the only racial slur still allowed in such "thoughtful and reasoned" company.

Many in the white working class are viewed as "the flyover people," the people of nonmetropolitan, small town, and rural America. They are the "unsophisticated," the "out of it" folks: the "hicks," the "country bumpkins," the "know nothings." Indeed, these locals are the binary opposites of those who are "cosmopolitans," who understand themselves as persons of "moral superiority, of informed knowledge, and of obvious sophistication." The opposites of these cosmopolitans are those who are antigay and progun, antifeminist and pro–white male, antiblack and pro-Confederacy, antiabortion and pro–American nativism, anti-immigrant and prowar. These are the stereotypes awakened in the minds of the new demographic of the educated, college-grad men and women, gays, people of color, the young, and most other progressives. All of whom should know better.

Barack Obama said about them: "They get bitter, they cling to guns or religion or antipathy to people who aren't like them or anti-immigrant sentiment or anti-trade sentiment as a way to explain their frustrations."[1] Hillary Clinton characterized half of Trump's supporters as "deplorables." She went on to describe this group of Trump supporters as "racist, sexist, homophobic, xenophobic, Islamophobic, you name it." She then added, "And unfortunately, there are people like that and he has lifted them up. He has given voice to their websites that used to only have 11,000 people, now have 11 million. He tweets and retweets offensive, hateful, mean-spirited rhetoric." She concluded this comment with the judgment that some of these people were "irredeemable" and "not America."[2] While both Obama and Clinton later apologized, they spoke out of a class bigotry that operates across a wide range of upper middle-class and elitist groups in our society.

Investigative reporter and activist Barbara Ehrenreich, who seems always so very sane and who has spent decades working for racial, gender, and class justice, writes:

> If the stock image of the early twentieth century "Negro" was the minstrel, the role of rural simpleton in popular culture has been taken over in this century by the characters in *Duck Dynasty* and *Here Comes Honey Boo Boo*. At least in the entertainment world, working-class whites are now regularly portrayed as moronic, while blacks are often hyper-articulate, street-smart, and sometimes as wealthy as Kanye West. It's not easy to maintain the usual sense of white superiority when parts of the media are squeezing laughs from the contrast between savvy blacks and rural white bumpkins, as in the Tina Fey comedy *Unbreakable Kimmy Schmidt*.[3]

---

1. John Pilkington, "Obama Angers Midwest Voters with Guns and Religion Remark," *The Guardian*, April 14, 2008, https://www.theguardian.com/world/2008/apr/14/barack obama.uselections2008.

2. Katie Reilly, "Read Hillary Clinton's 'Basket of Deplorables' Remarks about Donald Trump Supporters," Time on Scene, September 10, 2016, http://time.com/4486502/hillary -clinton-basket-of-deplorables-transcript/.

3. Barbara Ehrenreich, "Dead, White, and Blue," *Guernica*, December 1, 2015, https:// www.guernicamag.com/barbara-ehrenreich-dead-white-and-blue/.

Meanwhile Republicans and right wingers employ coded language and "dog whistle" rhetoric in order to make racist claims without specifically using "forbidden" language. In doing so they believe they can use cultural issues to blind these same people so that they will support candidates and legislation sold out to the rich and committed to avenues of action clearly to the detriment of all working-class Americans.

I do not know, however, which is worse: the cluelessness of the left or the mendacity of the right, the strategic blindness of the Democrats or the moral bankruptcy of the Republicans. Although, as we have seen, the complicity of the Democratic Party in its active neglect and opposition to the work-a-day, flesh and blood, working class is sheer hypocrisy, given the fact that it claims to be the "party of the people."

With these things in mind, what can we say about white working-class Americans? How can we get beyond stereotypes and get to some kind of flesh and blood representation of these folks? This is my aim here. To be sure, just as we must refuse to categorize them prejudicially, we must also avoid romanticizing them. Diverse as they may be, complicated as they clearly are, human imperfection and moral failure are theirs as well. The inequalities and alienation of class do not rid one of the captivities of race, gender, orientation, idolatrous nationalism, and the rest. And those of us not in the working class would do well not to scapegoat these Americans as guiltier of these systemic incarcerations than we ourselves.

JOHN AND EDNA STANFORD

In 1980 JOHN STANFORD married Edna when they were both twenty years old. In five years they had two kids, and he was busting his back dismantling cars at a salvage yard for eight bucks an hour. With Edna staying home to take care of the kids, he knew his junkyard job would not make it. Fortunately, he found work in a big corporate headquarters where he learned to install and maintain office decor and furnishings, which provided continuous work. After learning the trade, he set up his own business and had several clients. Clearing $70,000 a year in the mid-nineties, he was doing OK.

In 1997 his biggest customer asked him to come to work for them as their employee. They offered benefits, retirement, medical care, and a $55,000 salary. He liked the idea and the fact that he would no longer have the "headaches" of running his own company; he signed on. While he did not appreciate a kind of disrespect he experienced from management types in the office complex, it was good work, good pay, and good benefits.

In 2009, however, the business was sold to a German corporation that went immediately into a company-wide reorganization. They told John that he would be terminated, and, if he wished, rehired at a wage of $35,000 a year. They would keep him on the payroll at the lesser salary if he trained the new people they were bringing in. When the change in his wages took effect, John told them to stick it up a very dark place and walked out the door.

The Big Recession had begun. Out of work for a few weeks he took a night job in outdoor security for $10 an hour and no benefits. He was working five to six days a week and clearing under $30,000 a year. The kids were grown and gone, so Edna began working part-time in fast food jobs bringing in about $12,000 a year. They are getting by, but just barely.

They now live in a threatening world.

Hence, in this chapter I will do two basic things: First, I will report the way that pollsters typically define white working-class Americans and provide some of the characterizations polling studies find. While helpful, these broad generalizations need considerable attention paid to more specific descriptions. So, second, I will indicate the limits of polling and statistical findings in this chapter and suggest the necessity of examining significant ethnographic studies to attend to the diversity of our subject.

The "Largest Demographic" in the US

In his extraordinary book *Deer Hunting with Jesus*, Joe Bageant states that class warfare used to be "between the rich and poor" but that it has now shifted to a struggle between the educated and the uneducated.[4] This is certainly the way that pollsters generally work with class in the US. Of those twenty-five years of age and older, the class distinction is usually made between those who have a four-year college education and those who have less than that. Breaking class down this way makes the white

---

4. Joe Bageant, *Deer Hunting with Jesus: Dispatches from America's Class War* (New York: Crown Publishers, 2007), 26.

working class the largest demographic in the United States with 42 percent of Americans in this category—a group of such size that I am continually amazed at pollsters, pundits, and other social observers who suggest that they are losing their place in the larger society and in sharp decline.[5] That the white working-class members do not dominate the American demographic profile as they once did is clear, but to dismiss them as a powerful force in this society is a blunder of major proportions.

Using education as the chief marker of class, Max Ehrenfreund and Jeff Guo summarized the data on white working-class America. Below is a listing of some key categories of their findings.

- The majority of white Americans are working class.

- Almost half have more than a high school education.

- Ninety million have no college degree.

- Those with a bachelor's degree or more number 51 million.

- About 39 million or 43 percent have some college or an associate's degree.

- Forty-one million have a high school diploma.

- Nine million have no high school diploma.

- Median earnings in an ordinary week:

    - $706   White worker with only a high school diploma.

    - $1,154 White worker with a bachelor's degree.

    - $611   Latinos with only a high school diploma.

    - $611   Asian worker with only a high school diploma.

    - $568   Black workers with only a high school education.

5. Max Ehrenfreund and Jeff Guo, "If You've Ever Described People as 'White Working Class,' Read This," *The Washington Post*, November 23, 2016, https://www.washingtonpost .com/news/wonk/wp/2016/11/22/who-exactly-is-the-white-working-class-and-what-do -they-believe-good-questions/?utm_term=.5a495aca2bc2.

- Among white working-class men between the ages of 25 and 54:

    - 79 percent of those without a four-year college degree are working.

    - 5 percent are unemployed.

    - 16 percent are not working or looking for a job.

    - 93 percent of white men with a four-year college degree are working, with a similar pattern for women.

Ehrenfreund and Guo are quick to indicate that these white working-class people are not a monolithic group, and they certainly do not correspond to the stereotype of the rural, blue-collar worker. While these workers outnumber college grads in rural America, they reside primarily in cities and suburbs, not in rural locations; and, yes, the 2016 presidential election in the United States revealed a profound urban/rural divide. Nevertheless, 62 million of these white working-class Americans live within the larger environs of cities of more than 250,000 inhabitants. In these same metropolitan locations reside only 37 million white four-year college graduates.[6]

Education Alone Is Not Enough

The reason why so many pollsters use education as a proxy for social class is because of the sharp limits academic levels of achievement place upon a person's occupational future. For example, Andrew Levison reports that three-fourths of men with a high school education or less wind up in traditional blue-collar jobs, while half of those with some college find themselves in these jobs. As a whole, two-thirds of those with less than a four-year degree wind up in working-class jobs.

Among women it is difficult to determine statistically an accurate ratio between those who are working class and those who are white-collar workers "because of the huge clerical, sales and office category which

6. Ibid.

contains a complex mixture of both groups." Nevertheless, a "general picture" emerges with a third of women workers having a high school education or less, a third some college, and a third a four-year degree.[7]

Levison concludes that one cannot equate education and occupation as a definition of working class, but there is considerable overlap between the two.[8] Once again we have important ingredients of class that make the concept itself complex. An easy definition does not seem to be available. Moreover, when we add certain traditional descriptors of working class jobs such as hard work, monotony, lack of mobility, and close supervision, along with other characteristics of relatively low pay, few or no benefits, and little social status, the complexity of the concept increases all the more. All of this is to say that we must not make of the category of working-class people some simplistic template of beliefs, values, interests, lifestyles, practices, and other ways of being in the world.

The Trump Presidential Election of 2016

In the recent presidential election of Donald Trump, many journalists and pundits reported that the major factor in his election was an angry white working class, again suggesting a kind of uniformity not only of worldview but of politics among this large population. There were also suggestions that these white working-class Americans were no longer a dominant factor in American politics and hence were voting out of a resentment of their removal to the periphery of the cultural and political agenda. While I do not doubt that there is a lot of resentment and rage among the white working class, this overgeneralized picture will not do, and the idea that the white working class is no longer a powerful composite of the American electorate is simply false.

Early reports on the 2016 presidential election were informed by the Edison exit polls and were widely used by pundits and media

---

7. Andrew Levison, *The White Working Class Today: Who They Are, How They Think, and How Progressives Can Regain Their Support* (Washington, DC: Democratic Strategic Press, 2013), 43-44.

8. Ibid.

commentators. Defining working class as those without a four-year college degree, Edison estimated that the white working class constituted 34 percent or 46.5 million votes out of the 136.67 million total votes cast.[9] However, with the luxury of more time and a more sophisticated methodology, the Pew Center found that 44 percent of the voters were those without a four-year college degree and that they represented 60.1 million voters in the presidential election. This represents 13.5 million more votes than the Edison exit polls had reported.

Further, the Pew study found that 33 percent of these whites without a four-year degree are Democratic voters or Democratic *leaners*, which makes them a larger bloc of voters than the 28 percent of combined racial and ethnic minority voters without a four-year degree, who also identify with the Democratic Party. (Note: there is an additional 12 percent of college grad, racial and ethnic minorities not factored into this 28 percent.) These findings indicate that the white working class, so defined, is the single largest bloc of Democratic voters and leaners.

The Pew study also found a significantly smaller percentage of white voters with college degrees than did the Edison polling results. According to the Pew study college graduates represented just 30 percent of the total electorate, not the 37 percent that Edison reported, clearly indicating that white working-class voters far outnumber college graduates.

Finally, it is important to note that Hillary Clinton won 28 percent of the white working-class vote, while Obama won 36 percent of that same vote four years earlier. These numbers alone suggest that the white working class cannot be simplistically characterized as of one ideological persuasion and certainly not as politically impotent.[10]

---

9. A useful set of charts using the Edison poll can be found in the article by Skye Gould and Rebecca Harrington, "7 Charts Show Who Propelled Trump to Victory," November 10, 2016. See Edison Research for the National Pool, *Business Insider*, www.businessinsider.com /exit-polls-who-voted-for-trump-clinton-2016-11.

10. Thomas B. Edsall, "The 2016 Exit Polls Led Us to Misinterpret the 2016 Election," *New York Times*, March 29, 2018, https://www.nytimes.com/2018/03/29/opinion/2016-exit -polls-election.html. Also, see "Changing Composition of the Electorate and Partisan Coalitions" in Wide Gender Gap, Growing Educational Divide in Voters' Party Identification, Pew Research Center, March 20, 2018. For the full report, see http://assets.pewresearch.org/wp -content/uploads/sites/5/2018/03/20113922/03-20-18-Party-Identification.pdf.

Another study raises significant questions about the narrative that white working-class support elected Donald Trump in the presidential election. Nicholas Carnes and Noam Lupu note that most polls do not include data about how people actually make a living. Further, they show that most of the Trump vote came from affluent Republicans. Only one-third of his support came from households earning $50,000 or less a year; another third of Trump's support came from those making $50,000–$100,000 a year; and the final third came from those making more than $100,000 dollars a year.

Carnes and Lupu acknowledge that Trump's support came largely from those without a four-year college degree; but there are two problems, they contend, when class is based on education too exclusively. The first is that the absence of a four-year degree does not necessarily make one a part of the working class. (Consider billionaires Bill Gates and Mark Zuckerberg, they suggest, who are hardly working class.) Second, they remind us that the overwhelming majority of Republicans (70 percent) don't have four-year college degrees. Further, with two-thirds of Trump's vote coming from those making more than $50,000 a year in income, almost 60 percent of those within that two-thirds without a four-year degree had household incomes in excess of $100,000 a year.[11] Finally, this distribution of votes reflects the Republican base. In that sense, it is not unusual.

The Diversity of the White Working Class

These findings indicate that the white working class in the United States cannot be simply equated with those lacking a college degree. Not only that, it must not be stereotyped into some simplistic template of false consciousness and right-wing extremist views seen as the carriers of racism and sexism. Let us begin by looking closely at moving the diversity of

11. Nicholas Carnes and Noam Lupu, "It's Time to Bust the Myth: Most Trump Voters Were Not Working Class," *The Washington Post*, June 5, 2017, https://www.washingtonpost.com/news/monkey-cage/wp/2017/06/05/its-time-to-bust-the-myth-most-trump-voters-were-not-working-class/?utm_term=.7166075682c6.

white working-class people in this country.[12] There can be little question that there are significant regional, educational, wage, and occupational differences, not to mention variations, in the nature of the work they do.

My approach here will be to select some of the best research I can find on the white working class as found in different parts of the United States. These selections do not encompass the great range of differences to be found among white working-class Americans across the country; but they will display significant differences that need to be taken into account, so that what follows will be considerations of white working-class people in areas such as Newark, New Jersey; Youngstown, Ohio; Lake Charles, Louisiana; a small town in Northern California; and small towns in rural Wisconsin. I shall also consider anthropological research on a honky-tonk in Lockhart, Texas and an ethnographic study of a Jerry Falwell–loyal church in Worcester, Massachusetts, as well as other places along the way.

I do not expect to arrive at some essence of white working-class life that would provide a tool kit for ministry or community action that can be applied in every location and situation, but rather to provide a range of resources useful in working with and for white working-class people in ways that respect their indigenous ways of life.

To be sure, criticism of white working-class life is as necessary as appreciation is for their struggle and their often heroic lives. In my concern to appreciate the indigenous lives of the white working-class world, it is not my intent simply to be accommodative to what is there. Sharp, substantive criticism is necessary to their own well-being as well as the search for the common good. Even so, I hope that my critique will not be "external" but rather sensitive to the positive offerings that are already theirs.

12. Colin Woodard's book, *American Nations: A History of the Eleven Rival Regional Cultures of North America* (New York: Penguin Books, 2011), names some eleven regional cultures that make up North America. His book is an intriguing discussion of the histories of, and differences between, these rival regions, which he gives names such as "Yankeedom," "New France," "Greater Appalachia," "Deep South," the "Far West." and so on. Woodard's description of these cultures is stimulating and worth serious consideration, but I suspect they are not entirely accurate. But he does alert us to the need to take sub-regional differences seriously. In this book I will attempt to do this by selecting studies from different sections of the United States.

So, the job is to name the demons of working-class life without scape-goating, to identify false consciousness, and to appreciate the wisdom of people whose proverbs and stories are like sledgehammers pounding home some intimate or humorous or compelling account of a situation often not available to more established discourse. The job is to praise authentic ways to be a man without being anti-woman and to respect and appreciate those women who struggle not so much with a glass ceiling but with concrete floors at work and sticky linoleum at home. It is to recognize the sacrifice made by families without endorsing a whiplash type of politics that is destructive to their very lives. It is to claim a white identity that rejects supremacy and opens its arms to that rainbow of human colors that resides on the horizon of what it can mean to be a new people. And, of course, it is to love one's country, without idolizing the nation, on a continent where the massive majority of us are "recent" immigrants and where even the natives in our midst migrated here some thirty thousand years ago. It is to challenge internal myths of the white working-class itself that in the midst of all this economic and political devastation that "we are just temporarily down on our luck and may be one of the super-rich someday," but it is also to scorch those claims of the privileged that the working class deserves its state because of their stupidity and sloth, that they have brought it on themselves. I hate even more the claims of the mindless affluent who "acknowledge" their racism but derive gurgling delight from their categorization of working class whites as "stupid racists," somehow claiming high moral ground in the status games of an achievement culture.[13] And yes, finally, the job is to reject the confines of a narrow religious piety and a stifling dogmatism; to open ourselves to that Spirit ever at work and ever committed to be with us and for us in all the daily struggles and vicissitudes of history until the whole creation across its billions of years finds its home in the glory and majesty of that ultimate realm.

---

13. I am indebted here to my editor's reading of this manuscript and his reminder of internalized myths of the white working class about being "temporarily down on their luck." He identified the views of some in the upper class who see working-class problems in terms of stupidity and laziness, and his label of "stupid racists" names exactly a dynamic in the language of the privileged.

So, who is the white working class? I will answer that question not with a definition but with descriptions—descriptions provided by down-on-the-ground, close-up anthropological and sociological research.[14] As intimated by the comments of this chapter, there is no one white working class in the United States. There are, of course, similarities among many people in the white working class; but these, too, require nuance and appreciation for variance. We have barely hinted at regional characteristics, for example; but there are real differences between white working people in Atlanta and the white ethnic diversities of Boston or Youngstown, Ohio, as only three examples.

With these things said, we move in the next two chapters to six research studies, each in different parts of the country in metropolitan, small-city, and rural America. In the next chapter we turn to Newark, New Jersey; Youngstown, Ohio; and Lake Charles, Louisiana.

---

14. I have been schooled in philosophies that are wary of definitions. As a result, I turn more to *description* with special attention to the way words are used and especially the variations in their usage. This commits me to addressing the etymology or origins of words, their social location (who is using them), as well as their variations of use.

CHAPTER 3

URBAN WHITE WORKING-CLASS AMERICANS

ichèle Lamont studied white and black working-class men in New-ark, New Jersey, and white and North African immigrant workers in Paris, France. In this chapter I focus on her findings about white work-ers in the United States. Her interviews were with those who considered themselves "lower middle class," not poor. They were "steadily employed" even though "their living standards [were] in long-term and uninterrupted decline." Success, in terms of a rising standard of living, was not likely for these men. Thus it was a significant time for Lamont to explore their estimates of identity, worth, and status.[1]

Lamont's study could be called an exercise in the sociology of bound-aries, because she examines how working-class men make distinctions be-tween themselves and others—how they draw lines of inclusion and exclu-sion: who is in and who is out. More, how do they see themselves in contrast to the poor and to upper middle-class business and professional people? To persons of wealth? To other racial and ethnic groups, specifically in her study of US white working-class men in relation to African Americans?

Lamont found that morality and moral standards played a crucial role in providing dignity and in determining boundary patterns for these

---

1. Michèle Lamont, *The Dignity of Working Men: Morality and the Boundaries of Race, Class, and Immigration* (New York: Harvard University Press, 2000), 2.

men. That is, moral judgments resulted in distinguishing "people like us" from those who were other. The white working-class men honored "the disciplined self," someone who worked hard, who was responsible, who provided for and protected his family, and who had personal integrity. Standards of evaluation such as these provided rationales for these men to compare themselves favorably with "people below" whom they perceived as lazy and who held the wrong values, like the poor and blacks.[2]

These moral standards also sharply contrasted with business and professional people whom the men see as lacking integrity and straightforwardness. In their view, these businesspeople and professionals are people who beat around the bush, who will never tell you what they really think, and whose decisions lack sustained commitments and loyalty. They are too dominating, too competitive, and too selfishly ambitious. The workers did, however, respect business and professional people who had worked hard and fought their way up but did not forget "where they came from."[3]

In keeping with this last comment, these white working-class men did not resent the wealthy, believing that such people had worked hard and should not be criticized for their success. They did not think that the wealthy had been dishonest, immoral, or deceptive in gaining fortune. Lamont observes that such views coincide with those people who believe in the American Dream, an ideal in which the distribution of rewards is seen as basically right, that everyone has opportunity, and that anyone who works hard can make it.[4]

Lamont asks why white workers make this morality so central in their view. In a compelling description she names seven reasons. The first is that this kind of morality reflects central themes in US history such as the Protestant work ethic, self-reliance, and American individualism. Second, she names the conditions under which these men work, which are often hard, demanding, body racking, repetitive, and boring. Third, these work settings are also places to develop mastery and to display competence. Fourth, hard work is a pathway to upward mobility and may be the only

2. Ibid., 102–12.

3. Ibid., 110; see pages 107–11.

4. Ibid., 103.

shot the workers have if there is one. Fifth is the condition of the post-industrial economy, a time of offshoring, job dislocation and loss, declining wages, and so forth. Sixth is the workers' high dependence on others not only at work but in their neighborhoods. They cannot isolate or insulate themselves from people who are different. They cannot move to privileged residential areas so as to run from "crime, drugs, and undesirable people." These men, therefore, have to be even more responsible to avoid the damages that come from times of inattention or even momentary neglect. Finally, these impulses to hard work and responsibility are also fueled by a "yearning for predictability" for some foreseeable order in a world that does not always turn out right.[5]

These moral claims of dignity and boundary definitions are part of what Lamont calls cultural repertoires. They include certain narratives of national history like republicanism, the American Dream, Manifest Destiny, and American exceptionalism. Some are religious, as in Catholicism and Protestantism. These cultural repertoires involve institutionalized or publicly available categorization schemes.[6] They are the stories, proverbs, ideas, images, figures, and so on, that form, influence, and often guide actions and constitute attitudes. They are the stuff workers think with; the things that inspire them sometimes to go beyond themselves. And, as already said, such repertoires provide a moral grounding for the boundary work of inclusion and exclusion in working-class life.

Let me say that I find Lamont's language of "cultural repertoires" to be helpful, and I realize she is working as a sociologist here. In the context of her book, it is useful and appropriate conceptual language. Yet, in connecting with working-class people we need different language if we are to work effectively. Rather than repertoire I would suggest terms like *warehouse, storage room, stockpile, tool kit*, or, maybe, just a *barrel*. For example, a community leader, a pastor, or an organizer may well talk about a barrel of stories and ideas, concepts and categories with which workers come at the world. In chapter 7 I will use Lamont's concept of cultural repertoires and suggest ways of doing change with working-class whites.

---

5. Ibid., 26–28.

6. Ibid., 243, 273n28.

The Post-Traumatic City

We turn next to a very different city with a very different context than that of the suburbs of Newark. Justin Gest's study takes us to Youngstown, Ohio, which he describes as a posttraumatic city where the white working class that used to be its defining reality has become increasingly marginalized, deprived, and now sees itself as a new minority.[7] Gest chronicles the history of the city, especially the time when it was known as "Steel Town, USA." During those years it was run by the steel moguls, the unions, and the mafia. These political, economic, and social characteristics created a dependency on the part of white working-class people and removed them from community engagement and the policies that centrally affected their lives. But these were prosperous years for white working-class people with good paying jobs, benefits, and safety nets. When they needed something, they typically got it in a system that operated on a quid pro quo basis, that is, through a bartering system of giving and receiving favors with the powers that be. The Democratic Party dominated the city and still does in the absence of a competitive Republican Party.

Then came the collapse of the steel industry with its move out of the country in the 1970s and 1980s. Steel had provided "not only jobs, but also housing, loans, supporting industries, philanthropy, and sites for political organization and social life."[8] In just six years fifty thousand jobs were lost and with them $1.3 billion in yearly manufacturing pay. By 1983 a fourth (24.9 percent) were unemployed, accompanied by large numbers of personal bankruptcies, foreclosures, "domestic abuse, substance abuse, divorce, suicide, murder, and, notably, the mass departure of its population." In the 1940s the city's population reached 170,000, but in 2010 it had dropped to 66,982. Further, in its steel town heyday roughly 90 percent of the population had been white; but, presently, roughly half

---

7. Justin Gest, *The New Minority: White Working Class Politics in an Age of Immigration and Inequality* (New York: Oxford University Press, 2016), works with both Youngstown and East London, England. However, for reasons of brevity and focus, my attention will be on Youngstown throughout this discussion.

8. Ibid., 10.

of its people are black or Latino, since these latter two racial groups did not or could not flee the city in the same proportions as white residents.[9]

A central concern of Gest's book is the role of deprivation and its impact on the political participation of white working-class people. He finds that deprivation is understood by white workers in terms of what he calls "the symbolic repertoires of social hierarchies." By a symbolic repertoire he means "the way a group represents shared experiences to explain social identities and social processes. These collective representations are derived from and reinforced by the meanings and values that groups have available to them."[10] The repertoires are further used, as we saw in Lamont, as ways of generating boundaries and hierarchies for determining different levels of status (who is above and who is below and who is more central and who is more peripheral) and definitions of inclusion and exclusion (who is them and who is us).

Basic to these symbolic repertoires is the American Dream with its conviction that working-class people have agency, can be self-sufficient, and that upward mobility can still occur, which Gest describes as putting "blind faith in the continuation of an economic reality that deteriorated with the steel mills in the 1980s." Yet, in spite of all the evidence that counters this dream, most continue to believe in it, convinced that hard work will be rewarded, "albeit with caveats," says Gest.[11]

Gest reports that his respondents carry on

> a near constant internal dialogue...to explain their predicament and the redrawing of social boundaries based on class and ethno-racial difference. Their rehearsal of their ever-evolving personal narratives with fellow citizens consolidates a litany of stories about heartbreak, desperation, disappointment, and betrayal—recounting the tragic steps leading to a world where white working-class people have been displaced to their society's periphery.[12]

9. Ibid., 81.
10. Ibid., 149.
11. Ibid., 155.
12. Ibid., 150.

Gest characterizes the importance of the American Dream for the white working class by stating that it resides in a place typically reserved for figures of such august importance as Jesus Christ and George Washington. This may require a certain reshaping of the American Dream or of their own difficult times, but they do hold on to that dream.[13]

A basic part of the problem here is that when the white working-class people render blame for present-day hard economic times, they do not typically give structural reasons for the decline of a city such as Youngstown. In contrast with African Americans, Gest observes that white working-class symbolic repertoires do not offer "access to...*collective* [my emphasis] cultural resources and subsequently tend to embrace a more individualistic moral code."[14] Therefore, whiteness serves as a "burden" or "mark of inferiority" often leading white people to believe that they as individuals have failed to reach some meritocratic standard, a finding that Gest finds corroborated by other research.[15] Thus white working-class people in Youngstown tend to blame themselves rather than the system.

Here, with Youngstown, is a case where individualism obscures the realities of class, stunts the solidarity of labor, and allows systemic and structural issues to go unquestioned. Further, the assignment of blame on the white working class is joined by both middle-class professionals and public officials not only viewing the problem as an individualistic one, but identifying deindustrialization as a result of worker incompetence.

But Youngstown was *never* as meritocratic as nostalgia construes. Gest points out that the history of the cronyism, corruption, and quid pro quo of labor unions, the mob, and the Democratic political organization offers a radically different picture of Youngstown's past, and that each of these institutions was "as bigoted as the steel manufacturers they attempted to keep in check." At the same time, Gest observes that when white working-class people blame themselves and do not honor the hard labor and the long hours of their work, they "desecrate the labor they glorify."[16]

---

13. Ibid., 155.

14. Ibid., 26.

15. Ibid., 156.

16. Ibid., 157.

Still, the American Dream seems to be an empty faith. Gest provides statistics that demonstrate that America is "one of the most unequal developed countries in the world."[17] It is now a nation where large numbers of people are, in fact, permanently bequeathed poverty or working-class standing. We are stricken with the loss of "social ladders" and "social cohesion." Add to these the increasing loss of a progressive tax structure, the widening gulf of academic performance between the children of the affluent and those of low-income families, and the leveling out of mobility between the generations. All of these factors contribute to a gaping distance between America's social classes. Gest here references Robert Putnam's conclusion that America is developing into "a caste system" where our country's children derive their ongoing class standing from their parents because upward mobility has been sharply curtailed.[18]

Youngstown's white working-class people did see "cracks" in their American Dream. They know hard work was not always rewarded, that some people take advantage of those who are industrious, that entitlements are in play, and that some people make it because of who they are or whose they are. They understand that the system is rigged, and not in their favor. They get it that people just get screwed. As one woman claimed, the only way to fulfill the American dream was to win the lottery.[19]

For my purposes, the most important finding in Gest's book is the relationship between deprivation and the political behavior of the white working class. He investigates three kinds of deprivation: economic, by which he means a sense of obsolescence and loss of financial well-being; political, a perceived loss of power and the failure of politicians to care about them; and social deprivation, the sense of being marginalized and no longer at the center of social importance in the larger society.

Significantly, Gest does not find economic deprivation nearly as important in its impact on political behavior as he did political and social deprivation. Basic to these white working-class people is a sense of being

---

17. Ibid., 157.

18. Ibid., 158. See Robert D. Putnam, et al., "Growing Class Gaps in Social Connectedness among American Youth," *The Saguaro Seminar: Civic Engagement in America* (Cambridge, MA: Harvard Kennedy School of Government, 2012).

19. Gest, *The New Minority*, 158.

"demoted from the center of their country's consciousness to its fringe" and feeling "powerless in their attempts to do something about it."[20] Further, the more marginalized they felt, the greater the gap between their expectations and their achievements; and the more they saw historically disadvantaged groups such as people of color and immigrants moving to the center of American life, the more these white workers tended toward the radical right and the support of the Tea Party or Donald Trump. Conversely, if an individual saw him- or herself more at the center of American society than these historically disadvantaged groups, that individual probably did not align with the radical right.[21]

Having reported research from Newark, New Jersey, and Youngstown, Ohio, we turn now to a Southern city—Lake Charles, Louisiana—to study the far right, white working-class Southerners, many of whom politically identify with the Tea Party.

Strangers in Their Own Land

Arlie Russell Hochschild is a sociologist of emotion, a subject she finds missing in much of politics. In her efforts to understand the Tea Party she visited Lake Charles, Louisiana, off and on, for five years. It was her way to travel to the heart of the American right and to seek to discover the deep story of these conservative Southerners. She wanted to understand that story as *felt*. She wound up with 4,690 pages of transcripts of her conversations with forty Tea Party members and twenty others.[22]

Hochschild's research was not focused exclusively on white working-class people, but significant numbers of them were included in the study. So, this is yet another case where white workers share similar points of view with those of different class stations. Here Erik Olin Wright offers an important observation that a person's class does not necessarily determine how he or she thinks, feels, or where his or her commitments are; that is,

---

20. Ibid., 15.

21. Ibid., 186.

22. Arlie Russell Hochschild, *Strangers in Their Own Land: Anger and Mourning on the American Right* (New York: The New Press, 2016),18.

class by itself does not determine consciousness. As Wright says, "Individual subjectivity is heavily shaped by the macro-social context within which it occurs." At the same time, argues Wright, class continues to be a significant factor and "sometimes powerful determinant of many aspects of social life." This means that class must be explored "in interaction with other social processes."[23]

Hochschild's book is rich in the attention it gives to key events in the recent history of Lake Charles, especially those involving its dominant petrochemical industries, the politics around them, and the views of Tea Party members in relationship to these. She is impressed almost immediately in her study with what she calls the great paradox. She found extensive ecological damage—indeed, at times, devastation—that petrochemical corporations brought to the city of Lake Charles, its lakes, bayous, rivers, and even the Gulf of Mexico, which lies about an hour south. The Tea Partiers of her study understand clearly what is going on with the environment of Lake Charles and its surroundings, but they resist government intervention, regulations, legislation, lawsuits, and other efforts at environmental protection.

Why? What's going on here? It is partly a deep distrust of government, especially the federal government. For these Tea Partiers, to bring the feds in is to give up more and more control, to engage in regulations that exacerbate that control, to affect negatively the business climate of the local community and the country, and to shut down jobs. Hochschild lays out the "logic" of these views:

> The more oil, the more jobs. The more jobs, the more prosperity, and the less need for government aid. And the less the people depend on government—local, state, or federal—the better off they will be. So, to attract more oil jobs, the state has to offer financial "incentives" to oil companies to get them to come. That incentive money will have to be drawn from the state budget, which may lead to the firing of public sector workers, which, painful as it might seem, reduces reliance on government and lowers taxes.[24]

23. Erik Olin Wright, *Understanding Class* (New York: Verso, 2015), 154.

24. Hochschild, *Strangers*, 73–74.

Hochschild sees these claims as "a red state logic," but the paradox travels "with being a poor state with a lot of problems."[25] Nevertheless, this logic is based on serious errors of fact according to Hochschild's research. For one thing, people overestimate how many oil and petrochemical jobs exist. The Louisiana Mid-Continent Oil and Gas Association estimates that these jobs make up 15 percent of the state total, but the US Bureau of Labor Statistics number was a much lower 3.3 percent in 2014. The reason there are now so few jobs is because petrochemical plants are highly automated, and while it may require many workers to build these facilities, it takes far fewer trained personnel to monitor gauges, watch out for problems, and provide necessary maintenance and repair. Further, 2014 was the time of the natural gas industry fracking boom, when industry-sponsored research predicted eighteen thousand new jobs. However, only a few of the jobs would be permanent, and 70 percent of those employed would be people from outside Louisiana. By far, the greater number of new jobs in Louisiana was outside the oil and petrochemical industries.

One might think that the oil industry would make important contributions to state revenues; but severance taxes, paid when oil and gas are brought from the ground, constituted only 14 percent of the state's budget revenue, much less than the 42 percent these taxes provided in 1982. Moreover, the lowering of corporate income taxes to provide incentives to petrochemical companies, along with other tax exemption policies, had a crushing impact on the state budget under Governor Bobby Jindal. Hochschild found that "oil was costing more to lure [petrochemical companies] to the state and, once there, giving less to it. Meanwhile, to pay for this, public workers were fired and the state debt—$83 billion in 2012, much of it in unfunded public pension liabilities—remained."[26]

Hochschild also discovered that while oil brought in some jobs, it drove others away, and suppressed sectors such as the seafood and tourist industries. The 2010 British Petroleum Deepwater Horizon explosion, as one example, severely damaged these industries. As Hochschild said, "Oil and seafood do not go well together." And the much-vaunted consumer

25. Ibid., 74.
26. Ibid., 75–76.

impact from highly paid oil jobs did not come through. The hoped-for local spending from these upscale salaries and wages did not trickle down but "leaked out." Many of the oil and petrochemical companies were foreign based, and top executives did not construct luxury homes in Southwest Louisiana but rather in places like California and Connecticut. Meanwhile, temporary workers—like Filipino pipe fitters and Mexican nationals with green cards—sent their money faithfully back to their families at home. One expert "calculates that Louisiana 'leaks' about a third of the gross state product, the sum of the value of all goods and services produced by the state."[27]

You may ask, then, why? Why do Louisianans put up with this outrageous domination, exploitation, and environmental damage to their state by petrochemical companies? Local people know about the damage going on. In fact, some of the people Hochschild interviewed were actively contributing to the pollution and environmental devastation as part of their actions on their jobs. Local people could see the contamination of their bayous and lakes. It required no imagination to see a sinkhole of thirty-seven acres in size caused by a drilling mishap.[28] Lake Charles people call the road that runs along the Mississippi River between Baton Rouge and New Orleans "Cancer Alley," and the great river itself has been polluted for some time.[29] Amidst all of these environmental hazards, families experienced increased cancer and deaths among their loved ones. And, sure, there were activists who rose up in protest, but they were no match for the power of petrochemical companies and their control over state and government officials. Lawsuits were largely ineffective because of the capacity of corporate lawyers to string them out indefinitely over time.

As stated above, the Tea Partiers of Hochschild's study named "jobs" as the reason for their continued support of the oil and petrochemical industry. However, Hochschild found in her research an underlying, or more pervasive reason for the strange paradox of their lives. She discovered what she calls "a deep story," a narrative that she describes as "a feels

27. Ibid., 76–77.

28. Ibid., 99–100.

29. Ibid., 62.

as if story." In other words, the narrative in Lake Charles is not a story about judgment or fact, but about "how things feel"—"in the language of symbols." Hochschild contends that it is only as we take into account the stories behind left and right political positions that we will be able to understand how the other "sees the world." In her view, everyone has a deep story, a "subjective prism" that shapes one's perceptions and represents one's "hopes, fears, pride, shame, resentment, and anxiety."[30]

To understand the story of the Tea Partiers in Lake Charles, imagine a long line of people going up a hill, over which is the fulfillment of the American Dream. The people in the middle of this queue are "white, older, Christian, and predominately male, some with college degrees, some not." Behind them toward the rear are "people of color—poor, young and old, mainly without college degrees." Because there are so many in the back of the line, those in the middle are fearful of looking there. While the middle basically hopes that those behind will do well, they, themselves, have worked hard, they've been in the line a long time, and movement up the hill is slow. It needs to move faster. Their patience is wearing thin, particularly as they watch closely those highest up the hill.[31]

Progress is central to the American Dream. It is about more than money and owning things. It's about doing better than your parents did and enabling your children to do the same. The people in the middle feel they have endured long workdays, layoffs, chemical hazards at work, declining wages, and pension discrepancies. That they have struggled and survived through all of this is a testimony to their character and a badge of honor. Fulfillment of the American Dream is just compensation for who they are and all they have done.

But those in the middle of the line still see themselves as only halfway there; and, as they look up line, they see people cutting in and being given preferential treatment ahead of them. They see African Americans benefiting from affirmative action and being given special treatment in college and university enrollment as well as apprenticeship training, employment, welfare payments, and lunch programs. Further, preferential legislation

---

30. Ibid., 135.
31. Ibid., 135–36.

and policies extend to women, immigrants, refugees, and public-sector employees. These Tea Partiers wonder where it will all end. They see themselves as having played by the rules, yet they have never received this kind of special regard. To them, it is wrong. It is not fair.[32]

The Tea Partiers feel betrayed. One of those betrayers, clearly to them, is President Barack Hussein Obama. In fact, he and his spouse are seen as line cutters themselves. Even the president's story seems contrived and fictional: his birth, his citizenship, his education in elite universities (who paid for that?), and all the ways he seems to back the other line cutters. Their suspicion—generated in no small part by the false claims of right-wing media—is that he is a Muslim and that he was raised up on the Koran, not the Bible.

She points out that in recent decades the road of progress promised by the American Dream has become hard to travel indeed. Not only has the American Dream been more limited to a small, wealthy elite, but the wages of workers and others have flattened when they did not decline. The Great Recession of 2008 cost people homes and savings. For the bottom 90 percent of Americans, the Dream lost its power as a result of "automation, off shoring, and the growing power of multinationals," with severe impact on the US workforce.

With these changes, the bottom 90 percent of American workers saw increased competition for work between white men and a growing number of "others" in the economy. It also brought loss of recognition, loss of being paid attention to, and loss of being respected. The white working-class men and women felt no longer honored. Economically speaking, they had a very real point. Hochschild reports the claim of economist Philip Longman that those born after 1950 are the first generation in our nation's history to endure a lifetime of downward mobility "in which at every stage of adult life, they have less income and less net wealth than people their age ten years before."[33]

---

32. Ibid., 137–39.

33. Ibid., 140–41. Hochschild is quoting Longman here. See Phillip Longman, "Wealth and Generations," *Washington Monthly*, June/July/August 2015, 3, https://washingtonmonthly.com/magazine/junejulyaug-2015/wealth-and-generations/.

Much more could be said in closing this overview of Hochschild's work, but two comments are in order.[34] The first is to remind us that her work is a study of members of the Tea Party in Lake Charles, Louisiana, only. Her work does not represent all white working-class people. In fact, she states explicitly that "not all white middle- and working-class men in this squeeze moved right, of course. But many self-starters, men who'd done well for what they had been given, those in evangelical churches in right-leaning rural and Southern enclaves, those who had emotionally endured—and the women who were like them or depended on them—were inclining right."[35] Her research speaks to the diversity of white working-class people, and the deep story of those in Lake Charles should not be generalized beyond the scope of Tea Partiers themselves.[36] At the same time her findings about the deep story of the American Dream resonate with those of Gest, that those who feel marginal and powerless and view minorities and immigrants at the center of things were more likely to move right.

Second, I suspect that readers have already made connections between the focus on the offended morality and the sense of unfairness these Tea Partiers perceive and the centrality of morality in the research of Lamont and Gest. The last four decades have brought bad times for most white working people in America—indeed, for everyone in the bottom 60 percent or more of the class structure, especially for people of color. I am interested in how issues of morality have taken center stage in the perceived hardships white working people face. This finding will be a major clue in how we proceed and will be confirmed in the rural studies we examine next.

---

34. Some may wish to argue with Hochschild's framing of the deeper story, but I found it compelling that when she went back and shared her view of the deeper story with her interviewees, virtually everyone agreed with her account. Hochschild, *Strangers*, 145–46.

35. Ibid., 143.

36. Ibid., 145–46. Hochschild does report studies by other sociologists that support her finding of the deep story among members of the Tea Party. See Nils Kumkar, "A Socio-Analysis of Discontent: Protest against the Politics of Crisis in the U.S. and Germany: An Empirical Comparison," PhD thesis, University of Leipzig, 2015; and Theda Skocpol and Vanessa Williams, *The Tea Party and the Remaking of Republican Conservatism* (New York: Oxford University Press, 2012).

CHAPTER 4

RURAL, SMALL-TOWN, WHITE WORKING-CLASS AMERICANS

We turn now to the research of Jennifer Sherman, a study of a small, isolated, economically-devastated town in Northern California. In "Golden Valley," the fictitious name she gives to this small town, she finds that morality is "a social force" that generates and upholds certain kinds of social divisions, a finding consistent with the work of Michèle Lamont. In a place the size of Golden Valley, Sherman found morality to be especially powerful, because "there are few competing cultural repertoires from which to choose."[1] She observes that people are constantly involved in a process of differentiations among others in which distinctions are made and by which social order is constructed.[2]

Even with few competing cultural repertoires, however, she found a plethora of discourses that attended significantly to symbolic boundaries. In contrast to Lamont's study she found few references to ethnic and racial distinctions because, she surmises, the population of the town is almost entirely white. She suggests that "being white, in and of itself, goes only

---

1. Jennifer Sherman, *Those Who Work, Those Who Don't: Poverty, Morality, and Family in Rural America* (Minneapolis: University of Minnesota Press, 2009), 97.

2. Sherman is influenced here by Michèle Lamont and Marcel Fournier, eds., *Cultivating Differences: Symbolic Boundaries and the Making of Inequality* (Chicago: University of Chicago Press, 1992).

so far."[3] In this kind of setting not many "axes of hierarchy" exist. Thus, morality itself takes on even more salience and becomes a ruling force.

Sherman clarifies, however, that these moral discourses are more like "a conglomeration of ideas." They do not come from "a single, coherent ideology" but come from a range of social, cultural, religious, and psychological resources. The suggestion here is that homogeneity "of any kind" can enhance the role of morality in social life. At the same time, the morality she discovered in Golden Valley came more from cultural than from religious sources; but, again, these moralities are diverse, contradictory, incongruent, and take multiple forms—and with some, religion did play an important part in their lives.[4]

Thus, the purpose of Sherman's book is to explore the various uses of morality as both a concept and a discourse, especially by these white working-class Americans who live on the margins of a postindustrial, globalized world. With all its malleability, morality can rationalize one's own conduct; it can decide "who's in and who's out"; it can provide symbolic assets in the struggle for dignity and respect; it can magnify masculinity; it can sustain social order; and it can enhance self-worth. The range of these moralities can exult in American individualism; it can express itself in the fantasies of a frontier culture; and it can advocate a work ethic based in manual labor, to name but a few. Nevertheless, in all of these, Sherman asserts that at its depths this morality resides in "shared cultural norms and belief systems based in the community's unique history and customs."[5]

What is so stunning about Sherman's research is the significant adaptive role that morality plays in the community's response to the loss of its lumber industry and sawmills, and the subsequent disorganization and disintegration of community life. Further, I am struck again and again by Sherman's finding that morality is not so much a compensatory response to the economic hardship of Golden Valley but rather an active way to respond and deal with the profound losses the town has experienced. As a person on the left herself, Sherman faults liberals/progressives whose

---

3. Sherman, *Those Who Work, Those Who Don't*, 6.

4. Ibid., 7–8.

5. Ibid., 10.

"neglect, ignorance, and indifference" prevent them from understanding the powerful role that moral discourse plays in these communities. In Golden Valley, morality stands at the forefront of political and cultural thought, and even more at the center of significant local changes.[6]

I draw from the rich findings of Sherman's research just four ways that morality plays not only a significant adaptive role but a transformative one as well. The first of these would be the role of tradition in the cultural repertoires of working-class people in Golden Valley. Sherman found that the word *tradition* is used to endorse new practices, new family realities, changing roles within the family, new understandings of success, emerging values, new forms of self-esteem, and the use of some part of the American Dream, among others. The word can be used, clearly, to address concerns that do have a history in the community, but it can also be used to legitimate new practices and developments, as we shall see. It can be used for certain continuities of local culture, but it can also be used to justify innovations.

As I read Sherman's work, I remembered the story of the farmer who had an ax that, he said, was the same ax that had been in the family for four generations. Over the years, the ax handle had been replaced six times and the head four times, he reported, but it was "the same ax." By the use of this anecdote I do not mean to dismiss the important role of tradition in both continuity and change. No living tradition is some lockstep uniformity across time. I love Alasdair MacIntyre's description of tradition as, in part, "a socially located, historically extended argument."[7] Golden Valley embodies MacIntyre's description.

The second place where morality was significantly employed in adaptive and innovative ways was around family life. As one might expect, the hard economic reversals Golden Valley experienced brought severe pressures on families. Rising up to meet these challenges was "a belief in the righteousness of the family."[8] Traditional family morality became a central

---

6. Ibid., 181–82.

7. Alasdair MacIntyre, *After Virtue: A Study in Moral Theology*, 2nd ed. (Notre Dame, IN: Notre Dame Press, 1984), 222.

8. Sherman, *Those Who Work, Those Who Don't*, 187.

theme in the community's response, around which social boundaries were put in place. Sherman observes that "the typical nuclear family" was traditional in name only, but it provided a well-being and dependability for those who grew up with neither. Making it inside the family came to mean success. Being able to adapt and sustain family life became a source of self-esteem and self-worth. Family values became normative and, through the boundary work that moral discourse provided, these family values became ways to enforce conduct and to influence decisions.[9]

Closely related to family values was a third impact that morality had in Golden Valley around the relationships between men and women. Before the economic collapse of the town many men had good paying, hard-working jobs with a strong masculinist image from which they drew significance as breadwinners. When men lost the good jobs and living wages, there was a crisis in masculinity, and radical shifts occurred in what it meant to be good husbands and fathers. Sherman reports that a new "family values rhetoric" came into being, one more in touch with the difficult labor market and economic situation.

A majority of the men in her sample became what she calls "flexible men." They became more involved in fathering the children, more open to shifting gender norms for their spouses, more willing for their wives to work outside the home, able to recognize their wives' financial contributions; and, with these changes, these husbands committed to a home life with their spouses characterized by greater partnership and togetherness. Without this family values rhetoric these "flexible men" would've met more pushback from their peers and would've found it much more difficult to arrive at the kind of success they found.[10]

Not all the men in her sample were so successful in making the transition; fewer than half of the total number she describes as "rigid men." These men not only refused to change but intensified their resistance. Threatened by the loss of their power and attempting to keep the division of labor between themselves as breadwinners and their wives as homemakers, these men, as a result, suffered from self-esteem loss, substance abuse,

9. Ibid., 187.
10. Ibid., 191.

and unsatisfying marriages. Their rigidity generated and worsened discord for themselves and their families and "tore apart individuals and the families they formed." It was especially difficult, Sherman reports, for women pressured to be "stay-at-home-mothers" in families where the husbands could not find sufficient work and adequate incomes. This situation led to serious family tensions, financial hardship, and power struggles.[11]

The positive changes brought on by the "family values rhetoric," of course, made significant gains for women. Golden Valley women took on jobs outside the home to compensate for the lower wages men made, and, in some cases, for male unemployment. The women were even willing to marry men without jobs. What they would *not* do was accept substance abuse and domestic violence, which in the new traditional moral discourse had become anti-family. These new "traditional values" made it possible for Golden Valley to take on more *liberal/progressive commitments* (my emphasis) on roles for men and women without naming them as such. In doing so, traditional values provided an opening for what were perceived as outside influences, like feminism. Placed in a cultural repertoire of family values, women's equality could be viewed as local, rather than external, alien, and unacceptable.

The fourth impact of these moral discourses was the way the working-class people saw Golden Valley as home. With their power to make distinctions among people and places, the moral discourses not only legitimated Golden Valley as the place to live but vindicated the choice. By contrasting their small town with the problems of urban America, the residents of Golden Valley took on moral superiority.[12] This pride of place offered self-esteem and personal success to its inhabitants. The people understood that they had not realized the American Dream, but under the circumstances they believed that they had effectively captured "some part of its essence."[13] Sherman makes it clear that these moral discourses were not insensitive to the gravity of the structural and economic conditions

---

11. Ibid.

12. Ibid. 189. Sherman is alert to the ways that the distinction-making capacity of a moral language can cover over an "embedded racism" and can hide antipathy and fear of racial, ethnic, and class differences. We shall attend to the issue of racism directly in a later chapter.

13. Ibid., 189.

they confronted. They knew they were in hard times. Yet these forms of popular morality enabled the working-class people of Golden Valley to adapt, to concentrate on the upside of their lives, and to make no few important changes.

For now, let's conclude this discussion of Sherman's research with two comments. The first is that her study focused on working-class people who were a notch below the economic standing of those studied by Lamont. Many of the subjects of Sherman's study were in poverty and struggling to survive in an economically devastated small town. While the moralities differed in content, nuance, and in responsiveness to different contexts, the white working-class people in neither of these studies can be adequately understood apart from the central role that morality played in their lives. Attempts to do community work, ministry, or church outreach must come to terms with the key role and powerful force of this finding.

Note that in Gest's research, symbolic repertoires took on an individualism that did not provide for social or "collective cultural repertoires" that might offer different identities and more protest and dissent. As a result of this lack, Youngstown white working-class people tended to blame themselves for their economic hardship. One wonders if a family rhetoric might offer a first step toward a less individualistic and more corporate approach. As for Hochschild's deeper story of the American Dream, an important start may be to address the problems with the American Dream itself. We shall return to these matters later.

My second comment is that as important as morality clearly is, it is not enough. Sherman makes this very point, and we will return to it in chapter 7.[14] For now, it is enough to say that directions for community work and action will find an important point of contact in the moralities of white working-class Americans. Further, it is hardly excessive to suggest that the rage of these same people is in part a result of an abject failure on the part of other Americans to take note of these cultural commitments and their (our) abject lack of interest even to seek to understand them.

More immediately we turn next to a study of white working-class people in the US at the state level to pursue further the role of certain

---

14. Ibid., 195.

moral judgments and their place of significance, or lack thereof, in popular discourse.

Rural and Small-Town Wisconsin

Katherine J. Cramer conducted research in small-town and rural Wisconsin from May 2007 to November 2012. Her research consisted of three or more meetings with a total of thirty-seven groups in eight regions of the state.[15] The groups varied by race, gender, and age, although she reports that male non-Hispanic whites of retirement age were overrepresented in the groups.[16] As a political scientist her conversations with these groups consisted of an attempt to draw them out with regard to how they viewed politics.[17]

At the onset of her research Cramer's focus was on social class identity. As her study progressed, however, she became increasingly impressed with how much place intertwined with class in the conversations with her research groups. That working-class people are rooted territorially is widely recognized in social class studies, but Cramer is saying more. She finds that people from various class stations share a consciousness that is decidedly rural, which takes on prominence as people understand their lives and their circumstances.

She names this outlook "rural consciousness," which she describes as a lens by which the people of her study view the world.[18] This rural consciousness plays a very important role in terms of how people "make sense of public affairs" and "understand politics." Moreover, partisanship is not the key factor guiding their political preferences. For example, it is not commitment to the Republican Party that "causes people to have these complex, intertwined understandings of economic justice, place identity, class identity, race, and values." She points out that these rural groups

---

15. Katherine J. Cramer, *The Politics of Resentment: Rural Consciousness in Wisconsin and the Rise of Scott Walker* (Chicago: University of Chicago Press, 2016), 29–31.

16. Ibid., 37.

17. Ibid., 37–42.

18. Ibid., 51.

contain a good many Democrats. Rather, on the basis of her findings, how people vote is far more dependent on how they "make sense of their lives."[19] In other words, identity is more important than party. Culture is more important than "interests."

Cramer finds three major components of this rural consciousness. The first is "a perception that rural areas do not receive their fair share of decision-making power," indeed, a perception that they are ignored by power elites and policy makers. Second, they see themselves as distinctively different in culture and lifestyle from the people who live in urban and suburban Wisconsin, and these differences of rural people are not respected or taken into account by people in the cities. Finally, in the distribution of public resources rural areas do not get what is coming to them. They do not get back in government spending what they pay out in taxes.[20]

In light of these components of rural consciousness, the residents of small communities in Wisconsin believe they are victims of distributive injustice. Many see themselves as people who worked hard and earned what they now enjoy, or, if retired, resent the fact that their pensions are becoming increasingly difficult to live on. These small-community residents have a sharp sense of who is deserving and who is not, based on those who work and those who are lazy. They especially resent public employees and teachers who earn more money than they do, and who, they feel, do not deserve what they receive. They begrudge universities, and particularly professors, whom they see as arrogant, and who do not seem to listen to people like them but rather actively ignore them. One rural community person described professors as people who "shower *before* work, not afterwards!"[21]

A politics of resentment figures prominently in the views of the people in rural Wisconsin. It's not only about taxes, government spending, aloof universities, the image of cities as places of wealth, the advantages urban areas enjoy, and so forth. Even the tourists are resented, because those who come to small-town and rural Wisconsin do not fulfill hopes for a revived

---

19. Ibid., 89.

20. Ibid., 5–6, 12.

21. Ibid., 131.

economy; rather, some build large houses in concentrated areas that set them off from others or, perhaps worse, simply pass through their communities without spending much needed dollars.

Rural resentment takes many forms from "uneasy feeling" to "downright anger." It can also be quite comical. Cramer tells the story about one of her research group members who jokingly suggested that she should buy a horse. When Cramer said she didn't have a place to keep him, the man recommended that she keep him in Madison (the state capitol and the location of the university) because "that's where they keep all the bullshit." After the laughter died down he reassured her that "all you gotta do is buy the front end of the horse, they got the back end in Madison!"[22]

The observation is often made that people like those in rural Wisconsin tend to vote for politicians and policies that fly in the face of their own interests. Cramer certainly understands this claim, but she maintains the wrong question is being asked: "The issue is not why the white working class is getting it wrong, but why is nearly every voter getting it wrong?"[23] I could hardly agree more.

The people Cramer studied were not being distracted by Republicans from economic questions by having their attention drawn to social and cultural issues such as abortion and homosexuality. Economic issues were very important to the subjects of her research, but these issues were interlaced with social and cultural concerns. It is not the deceptions of wedge issues, as such, but rather the capacity of the Republican Party to "tap into existing resentments toward particular targets." The Republicans provided "frameworks" that identified "the demons" that confronted rural people—not the affluent and the rich and their elected servants—but rather government itself, state employees, universities, and urban centers where the liberals and people of color held forth. The point is that rural people defined the "them"—the "haves"—"not by affluence, but by culture," and Republicans knew how to touch the resentments of rural people by playing to these cultural issues.[24]

---

22. Ibid., 84.

23. Ibid., 221.

24. Ibid., 222.

The rural people of Wisconsin have lost their faith in government programs. Having struggled for generations, they have concluded that government programs do basically two things: they help the people who don't deserve it and they raise taxes. In the small towns and rural areas of Wisconsin these are not answers.[25]

Another question: Are the rural people of Wisconsin getting the short end of the stick, as they believe? Cramer found that the evidence is mixed. It is true that three-fourths of the public dollars go to the more populous urban, metropolitan counties, but rural counties actually receive more money per capita. Further, with respect to the average amount each Wisconsinite pays in taxes, rural people pay less per person into government revenues than do urban residents.[26]

Still, this may not be a fair comparison because rural people have not only different needs but less capacity to pay for the services government provides. So, if the differences are measured in terms of need and ability to pay, rural areas have "greater levels of poverty, lower wages, and modestly higher rates of unemployment."[27]

Another pertinent question is whether the money is well spent. Does it actually meet the needs of rural people? There are many good reasons to believe they are not getting their fair share. The enduring, gradual decline of rural America has been going on for a long time, especially the struggle of its economy. To drive through the small towns of this country is to see closed-up businesses all along Main Street and many houses in residential neighborhoods around it in disrepair and deterioration. Farm policy has favored Big Ag, and the loss of the midsize family farm has rapidly accompanied these changes. Along with these and other struggles, rural communities face a diminishing tax base but are required by county, state, and federal law to provide services.[28]

With limited means for rural communities to protect themselves from growing demands and the changing national and global environment, the

25. Ibid., 223.

26. Ibid., 90–93.

27. Ibid., 93.

28. Ibid., 94.

difficult economic situation in these communities has been called the "rural disadvantage."[29] Add to that the challenges of providing education in increasingly sparse populations. Or think of those rural communities that turn to tourism and become playgrounds for the affluent, which has been a mixed blessing. Or those that become dumping grounds for toxic and other wastes due to "relaxed" environmental protections and regulations.[30] Most, however, become "unseen grounds" in remote and/or nonmetro counties; they are the wide open, flyover people. Along with all these is the *brain drain*: the closing of schools and hospitals; the loss of representation in state legislatures and Congress; and, the movement of adult children to cities for work and careers.[31]

Cramer concludes that "something important and distressing is happening in rural America in recent years, and the something is not just one aspect of life changing but is instead a confluence of many things that is contributing to rural residents' perception that their way of life is under attack." Cramer understands that very difficult economic challenges face urban America; still, the hard realities facing rural communities "make their perceptions of injustice understandable."[32] Cramer does not argue that rural people are more "right or righteous" than urban residents; her point rather is that "there are solid and understandable empirical reasons that rural folks might think that they are the victims of distributive injustice."[33]

Two last comments before moving on. First, I recognize that Cramer included people from a variety of class positions in her research. My summary here does not reflect working-class people or even white working-class people alone. It confirms again Erik Olin Wright's comment that class does not determine consciousness, but it does provide one more implement in the tool kit of working-class people. As we have seen here in

---

29. Ibid., 95–98.

30. Ibid., 100.

31. Cramer's discussion of the challenges facing rural communities is the best thing I have seen in such short scope. For those in rural ministry and/or otherwise working in town and country settings, pages 93–104 and their references are worth the price of the book.

32. Ibid., 104.

33. Ibid., 110.

relation to rural consciousness in Wisconsin, Cramer's book offers, if you will, one more resource for understanding what is going on with white working-class people and the rage they experience.

Second, it is perhaps obvious that the role of morality in the research of Lamont and Sherman resonates with the role of an intense sense of distributive injustice in the rural consciousness of the people Cramer studied. This not only underscores the significance of moral considerations in white working-class life in quite different parts of the country, both in urban and rural settings, but also in different types of rural settings themselves. Those who would consider working with, indeed organizing with, this important group of Americans, need to be quickly putting together repertoires—or better yet, barrels of indigenous approaches—to be used in the transformative work so highly needed.

Ann's Other Place in Lockhart, Texas

We turn now to anthropologist Aaron Fox's study of white working-class people at Ann's Other Place, a honky-tonk in Lockhart, Texas, a town located some thirty miles south of Austin. Fox, a guitarist who plays, sings, and writes country music, participated deeply in the lives and music of the Lockhart honky-tonk in his study. His ethnographic work, conducted from 1990 to 1994, captures a pivotal time for working-class people and instructs us not only about the importance of the shifting fortunes of their lives but offers significant perspectives on their relationship to country music.[34]

The people he studied were those of the post–World War II compromise. Most of them grew up between 1950 and 1975, a time of the Korean and later Vietnam wars. It was an era of anxiety and violent tumult over conflicts of race and class. Nevertheless, it was a time when many working families had secured middle-class incomes; when public safety nets existed for victims of the more rapacious impact of the market; and a time when middle-class white workers experienced dignity and economic power not

---

34. Aaron A. Fox, *Real Country: Music and Language in Working-Class Culture* (Durham, NC: Duke University Press, 2004), 320-21.

known previously in the annals of capitalist society. These gains came at a price, and that's where the compromise lay. To work in the advanced industrial world meant highly repetitive, monotonous, and routinized jobs. Substantial wages came from "stigmatized, mind-numbing work," and the continuation of unequal access on the ladder of class mobility. Still, this was a relatively good time for working people, at least those in the higher paying jobs.[35]

By the time of Fox's study, globalization had set in, and the Texans that gathered regularly at Ann's Other Place were quite conscious of the changes coming to their community brought on by NAFTA, the high-tech boom, deindustrialization, and the movement of corporations out of town and out of the country. With their proximity to Austin, these working-class Texans saw in that city as well the rapid changes coming on. With the location of the University of Texas there, Austin became a technological, postindustrial, highly commercial, and wealthy cosmopolitan area. In the midst of this hurtling change, the city's increasing relatedness to globalization processes shoved working-class people out to the suburbs and to rural areas beyond, like Lockhart.

At Ann's Other Place, Fox discloses the impact of these changes on the emergence of a new working-class identity. Permeated by a "pessimistic defensive anxiety," these Texans use country music as a weapon through live performance, oral art, and a rich inheritance of "ordinary talk." The music provides comfort and becomes a mainstay of social identity for the people at Ann's Other Place. Across the years these and other working-class people have been "commodified, folklorized, stigmatized, and mummified in American national popular culture." But the songs and stories of country music are like barricades hurled up against "the alienating progress of an uncertain global postmodernity." Powerful cultural forces—popular, political, and economic—demean working with one's hands, reject the responsibilities that corporations and capital have to labor, ignore the centrality of location or reject outright the importance

---

35. Ibid.

of place, and disrespect with an oblivious ignorance the depth and skill of the working-class craft experience.[36]

It is within this demeaning context that Fox discovered the coming of a new identity in country music, one that bonded with communities and ancestry. It was largely the biography of that generation or so of American workers following World War II. And yes, in the music one can find all the things so typically criticized, especially by those outside the working-class world and outside the country tradition: its commodity forms, mythologized accounts of the past, oversimplifications, fantasies about marriage and family, stereotypical "redneck" personifications, sexism, racism, redemptive myth about violence, overdrawn masculinist expression, sugary nostalgia, gooey patriotism, and insufferable religious pieties, to offer a short list.

And, yet, there is something more—really, a great deal more—especially in the live performance of the music, oral craft, vocal practices, conversations, and arguments at Ann's Other Place. Fox found these local practitioners to be quite alert to the commodification of the genre, but they were embattled against such pressures. In the litanies and liturgies of country music, and the commentaries and conversations about it and about working-class life, Fox found Ann's to be "a rare place" where live country music performance "was the object of a vigorous intellectual and practical communal passion, imagined in intergenerational terms as a *tradition*."[37] The music possessed an authenticity in these terms that could not be reduced simply to a consumerist spectacle, by taking on a legitimate indigenous character. Indeed, working-class suspicion of commodity forms became the occasion for an alternative understanding of what could be trusted as real and authentic about the music. For the denizens of Ann's Other Place, country music and the rhetoric and verbal arts displayed there were "the authentic representation of their social experience."[38]

I will limit myself to one example from the dozens that appear in Fox's book. It relates to a comment made by one of the regulars at Ann's Other

---

36. Ibid., 320.

37. Ibid., 319.

38. Ibid., 318.

Place who said to Fox: "You can't raise me up in a honky-tonk and tell me how to live." Fox observes that the line "drips with semantic and cultural resonance." This line is not addressed to Fox; it is addressed to those "social forces" that are external to working-class lives but are seen as seeking control by telling them how to live. It is addressed to those who inhabit higher stations in the class structure and who are seen as taking inappropriate freedom by treading on the lives of working-class people. Further, such a line is addressed to those "external higher-ups" (my phrase) and is meant to be heard by them. The line reflects the resistance of working-class people and is clearly a polemical word directed against class snobbery. The beer joint becomes the center of working class resistance.[39]

Honky-tonks such as Ann's are "sacred institutions, liturgically centered on country music and verbal art as well as the consumption of alcohol." They were can be compared to the fundamentalist churches that claim these same exurban highways. As Fox says, "The oral and musical forms that are ritually cultivated in both churches and taverns are, as it were, mutually intelligible, and an air of sentimental fellow-feeling is common to both spheres." One of Ann's regulars told Fox that he had made a lot of friends and met a lot of bums in beer joints. He then opined that the church can be the site of such meetings as well. Reflecting on the difference between beer joints and churches, this patron said, "I'm subject to do a religious song in a beer joint."[40]

Further, the "sacred" characterization of the beer joint also speaks to "the nightly ritual of musically mediated beer joint sociability, an hour saturated with reflection on the politics of working class experience." The beer joint can also be the place where men escape "female-dominated domesticity," although "in real life," says Fox, beer joints like Ann's "carefully cultivate an aura of domesticity."[41] In fact, many of these beer joints become places for families; not only men and women, but children as well—in fact, sometimes many children.[42]

---

39. Ibid., 221.

40. Ibid., 222.

41. Ibid., 223.

42. Ibid., 224.

The point is that these beer joints become sites of resistance to the dismissals and denigrations of external forces posturing a class superiority. At the same time, in the face of global powers altering people's lives and taking away the world they know, honky-tonks can be a site of unreality where people fantasize and attempt to remember a world that is gone. Even so, these settings can be arenas for the celebration of life, for the performance of musical arts, and for a tour de force of oral and aural practices. The honky-tonk can be a place of working-class solidarity and life together.

Fox worries about the demise of this scene, which he notes has "declined in coherence and quality." Many of the people he knew are gone now, spread out across Texas and the nation. Fox worries about the loss of this significant musical tradition and about the disappearance of "ritualized live music as a community building institution for working-class people" whose communities are already suffering and vulnerable.[43]

Two aspects of Fox's findings need to be underscored. First is Fox's appreciation for indigenous practices, especially those around sociality and resistance. These are practices of important energy and vitality, and resistance itself is an important practice in working-class life. Being able to work with this resistance is key to doing social change. Second, the demise of the honky-tonks accompanies a loss of mediating institutions in the working-class world.[44] This is an area for indigenous innovation that ought to be placed on a high level of priority. Class tends to show up in solidarities, and the institutionalization of these becomes key not only to identity but community building, community organizing, and coalition efforts.

So far, however, except for brief comments on boundary practices of inclusion and exclusion, I have not directly discussed racism and the influence it has on white working-class Americans. It cannot be ignored, and it must be challenged wherever it stands. At the same time the scapegoating of white working-class people that can hide the profound systemic and institutional character of racism among those up the class ladder must be confronted as well. These concerns are the subject of the next chapter.

---

43. Ibid., 319.

44. See Justin Gest's discussion on the issue of the loss of mediating institutions in his book *The New Minority: White Working Class Politics in an Age of Immigration and Inequality* (New York: Oxford University Press, 2016) 25–28, 142–43.

CHAPTER 5

SCAPEGOATING AND SYSTEMIC, STRUCTURAL RACISM

Typically, I find that racism is too easily reduced to prejudice, prejudicial ideas, attitudes, comments, "jokes," images, figures of speech, and, of course, racial slurs. All of these certainly participate in racism, but they do not by any means encompass the vast systemic and structural characteristics of racism in its most powerful and devastating forms. I begin this discussion of racism with the distinction between prejudice and racism for two reasons. The first is so that we do not focus only on prejudice but address the greater demonic reality of racism. This concern is not meant to diminish the wickedness of prejudice but to place it in the even larger evil of racism. Second, I find that the scapegoating of white working-class people is usually couched in terms of their prejudicial attitudes, which many of them clearly have; but, by avoiding the larger reality of systemic and structural racism, this scapegoating lets privileged whites off the hook, except when they do navel-gazing around white privilege.

As a graduate student in the early 1960s I read Gordon Allport's great book, *The Nature of Prejudice,* where he defines prejudice as prejudgment, coming to conclusions before the evidence is in. But he also says that when it comes to race relations it is typically misjudgment as well, or, as he suggests, "being down on what you are not up on."[1] Soon after that, I learned that racism is prejudice plus power, meaning that it is more than the range of misjudgments about people of color and a host of other targets, but that it is backed up by power: the capacities of power elites, social relations, organizational frameworks, institutional payoffs and penalties, law and social policy, and long histories and traditions that form us and determine how we conduct our lives.

Even so, the roles of prejudice and power require attention to the cultural and historical impact of white supremacy. Rooted in the colonial activity of the European powers as they spread across the known world from the beginning of the modern period, white supremacy has a long history in the West and resides deeply in the psyche and institutions of our civilization. In the United States white supremacy goes back to the beginning of the explorations of the New World and the establishment of the American colonies. It has a history of slavery, Reconstruction, Jim Crow laws, and even today, the "New Jim Crow" era, as Michelle Alexander titles our own time,[2] with its police abuse and the massive incarceration of people of color, especially African Americans. This history and these continuing systemic and structural conditions constitute an ongoing testimony to the power, persistence, and ingrained presence of its bondage. It is as if radon gas is seeping through the crevices of our country's foundation and continuing to contaminate our national life. I still find the notion of racism as "prejudice plus power" and the ongoing pollution of white supremacy, to be compelling in their explanatory capacity, but they need fuller description not only in terms of the big picture, societal-scale operations of racism, but also in identifying and naming the practices of racism within the conventions of everyday, small-scale, ordinary life. So, I will begin here with an important study of Ferguson, Missouri, which displays the larger systemic and structural factors in a telling account. I hasten to say, however, that this picture of large-scale systemic and structural racism could be exhibited all across the United States. Following

---

1. Gordon W. Allport, *The Nature of Prejudice* (Reading, MA: Addison-Wesley, 1954). See www.writewell.narod.ru/materials/the_nature_of_prejedise.doc.

2. Michelle Alexander, *The New Jim Crow: Mass Incarceration in the Age of Colorblindness* (New York: The New Press, 2012).

that, I will look at studies of working-class whites and racism, especially the small-scale practices found in recent studies we previously discussed.

Systemic and Structural Racism

Before we move into the Ferguson study, we need to understand how *systemic* and *structural* are used here in the big picture of racism. In his book *Poverty and Power*, Edward Royce argues that poverty is a systemic issue and then illustrates his point by drawing upon racism. By "systemic" Royce means "an array of interlocking problems," which are "cumulative, reinforcing, and causally interrelated." He then demonstrates how racial discrimination leads to residential segregation, which further exacerbates racial prejudice and contributes to "a dual housing market and a separate and unequal school system."[3] With these systemic issues come poor neighborhoods with deteriorating houses, which negatively affect people's health. These health difficulties squeeze household budgets, taking money that could be spent on improved housing options or better childcare or more adequate forms of transportation; or, without medical attention, the system contributes to *chronic* unrelieved conditions of ill health. Managing these issues of poverty, in turn, cuts into time for working, diminishes the energy of adults, and restricts the achievements of children in school. Further, transportation difficulties complicate childcare, harden sex discrimination, and, when reinforcing each other, make it all the more difficult for parents, particularly single moms, to get and hang onto a living-wage job. All these things together produce "high levels of stress and anxiety," which make the poor "inordinately susceptible to illness and disease."[4] These vicious circles each have cycles within cycles and as such constitute systemic racism.

---

3. Edward Royce, *Poverty and Power: The Problem of Structural Inequality* (New York: Rowman and Littlefield, 2009). Royce uses David Shipler's characterization of poverty as "an array of interlocking problems," which Royce then applies to racism. See page 268. For further elucidation of Royce's understanding of structural inequality, see page 17. For Shipler's concept of poverty see David K. Shipler, *The Working Poor: Invisible in America* (New York: Alfred A. Knopf, 2004), 252.

4. Royce, *Poverty and Power,* 17, 268.

Closely related to the systemic character of racism and classism are the *structural* characteristics and problems that are external to individuals who are downscale in social, economic, political, and cultural locations. These are *external forces* that shape "the options available," "the access to resources," and the "allocation of advantages and disadvantages," "the state of the economy, the contours of government policy, the climate of public opinion, and the pattern of social relations." In other words, Royce uses the word *systemic* to name "the interconnected and reinforcing relations" of a multitude of racist policies and practices and the way each of these effects and are affected by the others. By *structural* he means the social forces of the economic, political, cultural, and social sectors of our lives that work through those systemic *relations*.[5]

STRUCTURAL RACISM ON THE GROUND

For an example of the systemic relations and structural forces of racism, let's imagine the life of thirty-five-year-old Auletta Jackson. She lives in Kansas City where she finished high school, got married, and had two children. Her husband took off after five years.

She works two part-time jobs in the fast food industry making eight dollars an hour. Neither job is full-time because her employers do not want to pay for the benefits of a full-time employee. Her schedules at the two hamburger places vary greatly because her managers want her only during rush hours. She never knows from week to week what her job hours will be. She makes eighteen thousand dollars a year.

Her low wages are the result of the US Congress not raising the minimum wage since 2009. Further, when our local city council raised the minimum wage modestly, and when a citywide referendum raised it even higher with a 70 percent affirmative vote, the Missouri legislature nullified any such decisions by local municipalities or voters. A legislature that touts local control as a campaign tactic pays no heed to such things when it is contrary to the perceived interest of those who pay their campaign expenses. Mario Cuomo once observed that politicians campaign in poetry but govern in prose. He failed to say that today most of that prose is fiction.

5. Ibid., 283.

Auletta's mother, who is in poor health, is housebound. Her presence is important when the kids come home from school, but with an eighth-grade education her mother cannot help the children with their homework, especially math and science. So Auletta tries to squeeze in time, as she can, to tutor them; but approaches to math and science are different now, and she has forgotten much of what she learned in school. The teenagers attend school where three-quarters of the students are poor and dealing with the same challenges Auletta's family does. School funding is never adequate.

All four members of Auletta's family are overweight, brought on by a high starch diet, which is the best they can afford. Auletta's mother has diabetes, and Auletta herself is prediabetic. Their medical care consists of visits to a free clinic in a local church. Because the reactionary Missouri legislature refused to expand Medicaid, none of the family is getting the medical care they really need. Added to this is the fact that they live in a "food desert" in the city. The nearest grocery store is twenty blocks away, and the "food displays" in nearby gas stations and liquor stores are nutritionally deficient.

The family lives in a dilapidated house east of Troost, the historic location of the black community in Kansas City, and the result of segregationist practices at the local, state, and federal level, reinforced through real estate and banking practices for years and years. They do not have a car, and Auletta depends on public transportation, which requires a long walk in addition to a bus trip to get to her two jobs.

Such are the interlocking problems of race, class, and gender in their systemic and structural impact on one black family in America. Auletta is one person, but she represents a number of struggling Americans in the millions.[6]

With this understanding of systemic and structural racism, let's turn then to a study of Ferguson by the Economic Policy Institute (EPI) to see how these have played out in a contemporary municipality near St. Louis, Missouri. Written by Richard Rothstein, the EPI Ferguson study provides concrete examples of the operation of both systemic and structural factors. It offers a broad sweep of their impact in a racially conflicted suburb that has been in the national news and has remained in the national consciousness.[7]

6. I am reporting here the circumstances of a person I know in Kansas City. I have changed her name to protect her privacy.

7. Richard Rothstein, "The Making of Ferguson: Executive Summary," Economic Policy Institute, October 15, 2014, http://www.epi.org/publication/making-ferguson/.

The Making of Ferguson

National attention came to Ferguson, Missouri, when an African American teenager, Michael Brown, was shot and killed by a white policeman. This event brought vigorous protests, rioting, and considerable racial tension. During this time many people were shocked that Ferguson looked more like an inner-city ghetto than like the suburban area it, in fact, was. Once a white suburb, it is now characterized by racial segregation, high levels of poverty and joblessness, low performance by students in "overwhelmingly black schools, oppressive policing, abandoned homes, and community powerlessness."[8]

Attempts to explain the transition of Ferguson from a suburban white community to a ghetto-like, inner-city black location focused on the "white flight" of prejudiced, former residents, who abandoned their homes to central-city blacks seeking better schools. The typical news account indicated that African Americans found their way into particular suburbs such as Ferguson through the practices of "prejudiced real estate agents" who directed them away from more privileged, upper middle-class residential areas. Meanwhile, these affluent, virtually white suburbs maintained their privileged communities through the use of zoning laws that allowed only costly single-family homes. At least, this was the tenor and substance of most news explanations.

These kinds of media accounts once again reduce racism largely to prejudice. As Richard Rothstein says, "No doubt, private prejudice and suburbanite's desire for homogeneous affluent environments contributed to segregation in St. Louis and other metropolitan areas. But these explanations are too partial, and too conveniently excuse public policy from responsibility."

In Rothstein's searing chronicle of this history, the determining antecedents of Ferguson, St. Louis, and racially segregated metropolitan areas across the country, resided not only in prejudicial attitudes but in the

---

8. Ibid.

"explicit intents of federal, state, and local governments to create racially segregated metropolises."[9]

Immediately below, I quote only the basic findings of Rothstein's report, but his narrative goes on to provide in historical and analytical detail the basis for his findings. This summary, however, is adequate for our purposes to demonstrate that greater reality of racism, of which prejudice is a participant but not able to account for the larger ravages of the systemic, structural operations of white supremacy. In summary about the St. Louis suburb of Ferguson, Rothstein states, "These intents were expressed in mutually reinforcing federal, state, and local policies." Here are Rothstein's findings:

- Zoning came with racially explicit boundaries that created ghettos and slums within the city of St. Louis.

- Public housing projects segregated the once integrated urban communities by race.

- Private sector agreements that excluded African-Americans from residential covenants and memberships historically were adopted as public policy.

- Local governments subsidized white-only suburban developments, depriving black families of the home equity–driven wealth gains commonly reaped by white Americans in the twentieth century.

- Reduced and inadequate city services within "ghettos" further led to slum conditions in black neighborhoods, reinforcing the whites' assumptions that "blacks" and "slums" were synonymous.

- Local government overreach of annexation, spot zoning, neighborhood boundaries, and other policies were used to remove established black homes from "gentrifying" or emerging white/affluent neighborhoods.

- Urban renewal projects touted as "beautification" or "clean up" projects shifted ghettos to new locations but didn't address core inequities.

---

9. Ibid.

- Real estate developers were favored by local government regulators and financial sectors in a tacit and sometimes overt promotion of residential racial segregation.

- A government-sponsored duality of workforce development resulted in significant inequality in job descriptions, wages, and financial buying power, leaving new suburban homes out of reach for urban hourly-wage-earners.[10]

In further substantiation of his claims, Rothstein quotes the Eighth Circuit Court of Appeals, composed of three judges: "Segregated housing in the St. Louis metropolitan area was...in large measure the result of deliberate racial discrimination in the housing market by the real estate industry and by agencies of the federal, state, and local governments."[11] Rothstein goes on to say that conclusions like this one could be substantiated in large metropolitan areas across the nation.

Acknowledging that explicit policies such as those in the list are no longer lawful, "their effects," argues Rothstein, continue to operate in racially segregated neighborhoods in every region of the United States. He adds: "When we blame private prejudice and snobbishness for contemporary segregation, we not only whitewash our own history, but avoid considering whether new policies might instead promote an integrated community." Rothstein states that "a century of evidence" substantiates the finding that "St. Louis was segregated by interlocking and racially explicit public policies of zoning, public housing, and suburban finance, and by publicly endorsed segregation policies of the real estate, banking, and insurance industries." Further, he contends that these federal, state, and local policies acted in concert with "the public labor market and employment policies" to discriminate against blacks and close doors to jobs for which they were qualified. He then speaks to the way that "mutually reinforcing public policies conspired with private prejudice to turn St. Louis's African American communities into slums."[12]

---

10. Ibid.

11. Ibid.

12. Ibid.

Scapegoating the White Working Class

Racism must be addressed in the fullest account we can offer. If we misdiagnose or underdiagnose the depths or extent of its reach, we will not arrive at solutions adequate to challenge it and move toward a racially just society. Further, when privileged Caucasians scapegoat white working-class people as racist and thereby reduce racism to their prejudicial expressions, we miss the complicity of the larger society—ourselves—in its more encompassing and profound racist systems and structures. To explore Ferguson is to tour a microcosm of America.

Also important is recognizing that many working people are not prejudiced as measured by their attitudes, beliefs, comments, and actions. Many white working-class people work on jobs, live in neighborhoods, relate socially with friends, participate recreationally, and yes, marry and have children across racial lines. To be sure, this does not mean they are free from complicity in and with the systemic and structural forms of racism, but it does say that working-class people are diverse in racial consciousness, and that needs to be recognized.

Clearly, there are prejudiced and bigoted white working-class people as well, and this needs to be named and addressed. The remainder of this chapter will focus on two matters: first, on a brief look at the work of W. E. B. Du Bois and W. J. Cash and their important contributions to the role of racism with working-class whites; and then on recent research that moves beyond generalizations about prejudice and racism and focuses specifically on the granular practices of these in working-class life today.

The White Working Class and the Wages of Whiteness: Du Bois and Cash

One of the most telling insights into the racism of working-class whites comes from the work of W. E. B. Du Bois. He describes the tragedy of the labor movement in the United States as one where the rightful claims, interests, and actions of working people became divided by race. The problem for the white working-class was not merely that it got hustled into racism but rather that it found its identity and central interests in terms of whiteness. Du Bois understands that there was clearly a short-term payoff in wages and other material advantages for white workers over blacks, but in his analysis, he emphasizes that these workers perceived an even greater advantage in their white identity.

Du Bois called this advantage "the wages of whiteness." It was an added compensation, a payoff not in money but rather a "public and psychological wage." While this amounted to a gain in status, it provided other quite substantive advantages, such as public deference and admission to community functions and public parks. The police came from white working-class ranks; and the courthouse judges needing the votes of the white working class in elections, provided these whites with a certain leniency. To be sure, while their votes may have elected certain public officials, the franchise had little effect on the material improvement of these same white working people. Further, the public school buildings whites attended were among the best in their community and, prominently located, received tax revenue support two to ten times that of segregated black public schools.[13] Even more, the pleasure of being white operated as a wage for these workers so that the status and privileges of being white were employed to compensate for the alienation and exploitation that came with being working-class. So, workers, North and South, could claim that at least they were "not slaves" or "not black."

White workers failed to see they had common interests with blacks, such as they both suffered exploitation and oppression; whites were simply blinded by the fool's gold of a white identity and the rather limited privileges it provided.[14]

In 1941, W. J. Cash published *The Mind of the South*, a book that shares some similarities with the work of Du Bois. Both authors note that the status and privilege accorded to whites was used as a compensative and manipulative practice—used, in fact, against the interests of the white lower class—to garner their support socially, politically, and economically.

---

13.   W. E. B. Du Bois, *Black Reconstruction in America, 1860–1880* (New York: Free Press, 1997), 700–701.

14.   Ibid., 30, 700. For a use of Du Bois's analysis of the wages of whiteness, see David R. Roediger, *The Wages of Whiteness: Race and the Making of the American Working Class*, 2nd ed. (New York: Verso, 1991).

They were roused to be in opposition to the presumed threat of blacks and in furthering the interests of powerful whites.[15]

Cash argues that class was not a significant tradition in the development of the plantation South and its aftermath. The Southerner was a rustic figure, "a direct product of the soil," characterized by an intense individualism. Possessing distrust of the state, and of authority more generally, Southerners were more shaped by the tradition of the backcountry and the plantation. Because of an intense "community of feeling" in the white population and "an immense kindliness and easiness" (Southern manners, etiquette), white farmers and poor whites perceived plantation owners as "kinsman." Further, claims Cash, the widespread use of slavery on the plantations meant that lower-class whites were not needed for labor and were able to gain land, subsistence, and freedom, albeit not to match the scale of the plantation owners. But still they "escaped servitude."[16]

With respect to black slaves, lower-class white Southerners had the "vastly ego-warming and ego-expanding distinction" between the two races.[17] No matter that these lower-class whites were often robbed and degraded by powerful plantation interests; they nevertheless had status as white people. Not so much exploited directly, these whites were "made by extension a member of the dominant class" and "lodged solidly on a tremendous superiority." No matter what happened, in their eyes they would forever be white. Moreover, Cash observes, even with their own leisure "reamed out," they despised "nigger work" and gained a sense of position, standing, and white superiority by the fact they were not black and would always be white.[18]

---

15. W. J. Cash, *The Mind of the South* (New York: Vintage Books, 1991).

16. Ibid, 30–35.

17. Ibid., 38–39.

18. Ibid, 48–49. On pages 425–26 of *The Mind of the South*, Cash offers a comment that many believe summarizes his argument in the book: "Proud, brave, honorable by its lights, courteous, personally generous, loyal, swift to act, often too swift, but signally effective, sometimes terrible, in its action—such was the South at its best. And such at its best it remains today, despite the great falling away in some of its virtues. Violence, intolerance, aversion and suspicion toward new ideas, an incapacity for analysis, an inclination to act from feeling rather than from thought, an exaggerated individualism and too narrow concept of social responsibility, attachment to fictions and false values, above all too great attachment to racial values and a tendency to justify cruelty and injustice in the name of those values, sentimentality and a lack of realism—these have been its characteristic vices in the past. And, despite changes for the better, they remain its characteristic vices today."

The work of Du Bois and Cash are of signal importance in understanding the dynamics of racism. There can be no question that the role of white supremacy in the United States is, in part, a function of the compensative functions that each of them identifies. At the same time, racism and white supremacy are complex and complicated. There is more going on, at least in forms of oppression, than only a compensative function. If we are to respond adequately to racism, especially in the white working class, then we must examine the dynamics of what is currently operative. My thought is that this will give us new avenues of direction and action. For this reason, we will revisit the studies of Lamont, Gest, Hochschild, Sherman, and Cramer.[19]

Morality, Boundaries, Distinctions, and Racial Rhetoric

In Lamont's study we saw the central role of morality in setting up boundaries, distinctions, and criteria of inclusion and exclusion, which also differentiated the deserving from the undeserving. Thus, morality was partly a categorization scheme that constituted a range of concepts by which the world was understood and engaged. The ideas, images, narratives, and so on constituted a reservoir of cultural resources by which white working-class people attended to issues of dignity, identity, family stability, community, those who were other, and racism.

In these terms morality plays a specific role in what Lamont calls the "rhetoric of racism." That is, "Whites and blacks alike subtly move from drawing moral boundaries to drawing racial boundaries."[20] With white men these moral standards were central to their concept of the

---

19. We will not consider Fox's work in this section on racism, since it does not offer direct avenues for dealing with racism. In Fox's study, Ann's Other Place was not a segregated honky-tonk, but "subtle forms of racialized hierarchy persisted"; Aaron A. Fox, *Real Country: Music and Language in Working-Class Culture* (Durham, NC: Duke University Press, 2004), 26–27.

20. Michèle Lamont, *The Dignity of Working Men: Morality and the Boundaries of Race, Class, and Immigration* (Cambridge, MA: Harvard University Press, 2000), 93–96. I question Lamont's use of the word *racism* to characterize the prejudices of African Americans. I reserve the word *racism* for circumstances in which racial *privilege*, discrimination, and segregation participate in much larger systemic and structural formations. Black prejudice, which certainly exists, does not have the powerful backing of the larger society in these systemic and structural terms.

"disciplined self," which characterized their ideal and cast blacks in violation of its aims. Blacks, in turn, found whites transgressing on their ideal of the "caring self." Whites lacked compassion, and were too domineering, competitive, and imperialistic, as well as less human, spiritual, and morally courageous, given their incapacity to deal with hardship.[21]

While not attempting to justify the "racist rhetoric" in these contrasting white and black views, Lamont works with these sorts of rhetoric to discover their internal coherence and to ask why these contrasting views make sense to the two respective groups. Her answer to this question is quite revealing. She found that the moral standards of white working-class men revolved around "a work ethic, responsibility, and the defense of traditional morality," largely focused around family values and anti-crime commitments.

Basic to her point is that white working-class men approach racial differences, not through racism per se, but rather through the framework of their "general moral world views."[22] For example, she reports the general finding that patriotism is associated with classical racism in the white working class; that is, they see blacks as detrimental to the best America has to offer. This suggests a social change approach initially, not to racism but to *patriotism*—an approach to social change I will discuss on behalf of justice for working-class whites.

Lamont also found anti-racist arguments among white working-class men. These arguments decidedly did not use those of multiculturalism and diversity, popular among the university trained. Instead, the arguments of the white working men were around the capacity of blacks to have good earning capacity, "a reflection of the productivity/Republican tradition." Moreover, all people were understood to share a common human nature

---

21. Ibid., 93. Lamont found that African Americans viewed work as a source of identity, saw themselves as "decent people," and held in high regard those who "keep on," who do not give up, who get up early, and work very hard to provide food for their families. While they did not put work at the center of their identity, as 20 percent of the white workers did, they did define worth through morality; they "simply put most emphasis on the other dimensions of morality (the caring self)." Their understanding of morality "overlaps with, but also differs from, that of whites." By no means, however, did black workers see themselves as morally deficient with respect to whites (see 28–29).

22. Ibid., 72.

and a common lineage ("we all need to eat" or "the poor are like us"). Further, this anti-racist rhetoric maintained that there were good and bad people in all races. As one man said, "It does not matter if you are black or white, or pink or purple, or yellow or green. If you are a miserable SOB, you're just a miserable SOB, no matter what color you are."[23]

Lamont's work offers a number of key resources for addressing racism among working-class whites. Her concept of cultural repertoires, the role of morality in making distinctions and generating principles of inclusion and exclusion, the place of dignity, identity, symbolic boundaries, and the possibilities for change through these dynamics are all important for addressing the issue of racism as we shall develop later. Moreover, the use of anti-racist arguments already in place among some white workers is an important avenue for support and expansion.

From Lamont's study it is clear that the arguments of Du Bois and Cash, as important as they are, do not address the complexity of the cultural repertoires of contemporary white working-class men. The cultural ingredients in the repertoires of these men are more complicated and offer more nuance than the role of whiteness as only compensative. The good news is that a fuller diagnosis of where we are today provides more avenues for working with white working people on the issue of racism. Before turning to that matter, however, we will explore other studies to continue to build a larger repertoire of cultural resources that can be rightly used in white working-class communities.

Deprivation and Living on the Fringe

In Youngstown Gest found diversity of political views among the white working class, but he discovered that those who experienced loss of power and status and resented the perceived gains of minorities and immigrants were those most likely to move to the extreme right. In contrast, those less deprived, less consigned to the margins of the community, and not resentful of minorities and immigrants were less likely to do so. Gest's central point here is that powerlessness, marginality, and resentment, and

23. Ibid., 70. See also pages 248–49.

their key role in racism and political commitments, are even more important than economic loss.

Racism and the American Dream

In Hochschild's work on the Tea Party in Lake Charles she deals with racism primarily centered around her discussion of the deeper story of the long line going up the hill to the American Dream. These Tea Partiers denied being racist, and "by their own definition, they clearly were not...a person who used the 'N' word or who 'hates' blacks," says Hochschild. If, however, one means by racism "the belief in a natural hierarchy that places blacks at the bottom and the tendency of whites to judge their own worth by distance from the bottom," Hochschild states, then "many Americans, north and south, are racist." She also indicates that racism includes more than "personal attitudes" but must take into account structural arrangements as well.[24]

Hochschild also observes the isolation that most of her respondents had from African Americans and therefore the lack of close contact with them. She found that their images of blacks came from three places: first, the wealthy and famous "megastars of music, film, and sports"; second, those who "were a disproportionate part of the criminal class"; and, third, welfare recipients. Absent from these images was a black person "standing patiently" next to them in that line up the hill to the American Dream. That is, she heard no comment about African Americans sharing the Tea Party respondent's circumstance of "waiting for a well-deserved reward."[25]

Morality as Adaptive and Transformative

The relevance of Sherman's research does not address racism directly because she found few racial/ethnic references in her year's residence in the small town of Golden Valley. Yet, like Lamont, she found morality to be of

---

24. Arlie Russell Hochschild, *Strangers in Their Own Land: Anger and Mourning on the American Right* (New York: New Press, 2016), 146–47.

25. Ibid., 147.

utmost significance in its contribution to social order, the drawing of symbolic boundaries, and the making of distinctions between "them and us." Most valuable for our immediate purposes in addressing racism is the implications of her research on morality, not only for its adaptive functions, but for the transformative role it can play. Her work demonstrates that traditional values and commitments can bring about significant change in the development of new practices and new relationships. Calling upon tradition, working with notions of family life, reworking relationships between men and women, and using pride of place and location become, in her findings, not sources of rigidity and failure, but rather significant ways to cope with a challenging context and turn it in a new, more viable direction. This should give us some idea of a more indigenous—in the good sense—approach to social change and communities that share at least some of the characteristics of Golden Valley.

Racism and Rural Consciousness

Cramer's research in rural and small-town Wisconsin offers yet another account of racism. As with other research on the white working class she finds that identity was central to the determination of how they voted, and a central feature of rural consciousness, which inevitably involved what rural Wisconsinites saw as the role government should play. As they understood this role they made a sharp distinction between rural and non-rural people, seeing the latter as people who were not committed to hard work and who held different values. This boiled down to who was deserving and who was not; who was "them" and who was "us." The evaluation of a given government program depended on who its beneficiaries were seen to be.

Cramer asks the question whether racism is involved when people object to the taxing of their "hard-earned dollars" to provide unjust government programs in the city. She says, "The answer is not a simple yes." She acknowledges that racism underpins a good deal of the opposition to government spending, especially welfare, but some studies contend that this opposition is "based on the principle of individualism, not rooted in racist beliefs."[26] Further, historically, since the Progressive Era (1800s to 1920s) the city has stood for a combination of both government expansion and diversity together in the popular imagination. Finally, race has been used directly or indirectly to gain support for or opposition to various candidates, legislation, and other policy matters; and, clearly, racial stereotypes have played a significant role in these political struggles.

Still, Cramer is hesitant to account for rural consciousness as simply an expression of racism. Part of her reluctance is because today "'racism' is often understood as blatant discrimination against people of color," but this is not what she found among the subjects of her study. In fact, *she did not find one comment* (emphasis is mine) in her field notes where a rural person named an urban dweller as being a lazy welfare beneficiary. While she found several such comments among city and suburban residents, she "found exactly zero such exchanges in rural communities."[27]

Rather, what Cramer found with rural residents were complaints about the cities receiving many more tax dollars and services than rural areas. When they discussed "those people on welfare," their comments were aimed at their white neighbors, not urban people of color. And when the rural residents talked about lazy people in the cities, they were targeting government employees, people of wealth, and often young people—all of whose work was, quite apparently to these rural Wisconsinites, less arduous than their own.

Cramer understands, however, that racism is complicated today. It cannot be explicated from either residence or class in this country. Centuries-long discrimination inevitably "colors our impressions of what kind of people are where and our willingness to share resources with them." Cramer sees quite clearly the way that politicians manipulate racism and racist stereotypes to generate resentment and to sharpen opposition to redistributive government spending.[28]

---

26. Katherine J. Cramer, *The Politics of Resentment: Rural Consciousness in Wisconsin and the Rise of Scott Walker* (Chicago: University of Chicago Press, 2016), 165.

27. Ibid., 166.

28. Ibid.

She also reminds us that many people in our country are having a hard time and believe that government is neither listening nor responding to their plight. If people were to blame those whom government policies actually privilege—the affluent and wealthy—she claims, the aim of rural resentment would not perhaps be toward "the undeserving poor," "the indolent," and "overpaid" government employees. Should this happen, they might favor progressive taxation, campaign spending reform, and adequate safety nets for those in need. But our country is under the grip of right-wing power, and Cramer concludes with these words: "To be blunt: conservative politicians encourage people to focus on the undeserving as a way to achieve their goal of limiting government without harming the interests of the wealthy."[29]

In response to Cramer's research there are significant learnings about rural people in Wisconsin that name repertoires of cultural resources that must be taken into account, according to context, in the struggle against racism. Specifically, in Cramer's study, dealing with racism in the white working class requires attention to morality or conceptions of distributive injustice; the issue of identity; the targets of resentment; the importance of place; the role of hard work; and sensitivity to rural consciousness, which does not typically refer to the realities of class.

We are almost ready to turn our attention to strategies of change in white working-class communities in the United States. One other study, not yet considered here, however, offers additional contributions to this endeavor, with findings in Boston and Atlanta, thus providing further regional settings important to our considerations.

Racism in Boston and Atlanta: The Diversity of Its Forms

Monica McDermott spent a year studying racism, roughly dividing her time between Boston, Massachusetts and Atlanta, Georgia. To conduct her research, she worked as a clerk in a convenience store in each of the two cities in a white working-class neighborhood that bordered a

---

29. Ibid., 167.

black community. Her findings are important not only to display contrasts between Boston and Atlanta but also to offer nuance and expose differences of racism we have not yet considered.[30]

McDermott brings to her study an important question regarding what appears to be increasing tolerance and liberalism regarding race, as shown in public opinion polls in the United States, and the fact that these poll findings continue to be accompanied in the larger society by persistent segregation in schools and residential areas, different political opinions and party identifications, and recurring outbreaks of violence between blacks and whites. Her participant observation approach is an attempt to move into what she calls "micro-situations" so that she might get a closer look at relationships and practices between blacks and whites, specifically those occurring in and around the two convenience stores where she was employed.

Not surprisingly, she found that "anti-black prejudice is alive and well." While "race is far from an obsession for most whites," it is unusual for whites to talk about race if African Americans are around and with people they don't know, of whatever color. Whites do not typically make negative comments about blacks; nevertheless, she found that certain situations and particular topics—such as sex, crime, neighborhoods, schools, and black men—brought out racial stereotypes and denigrative comments. McDermott believes that her working and living in the community gave her access to the "interracial antipathy" and "its limits," which she otherwise would not have known.[31]

I want to lift up basically six findings from McDermott's research that bear directly upon our interest in finding clues for addressing racism among white working-class Americans. These six findings, however, certainly will not exhaust the rich detail of her work, which deserves significant attention in itself.

---

30. Monica McDermott, *Working-Class White: The Making and Unmaking of Race Relations* (Berkeley: University of California Press, 2006), 149–51. McDermott is using here a concept from Randall Collins, "Situational Stratification: A Micro-Macro Theory of Inequality," *Sociological Theory* 18 (2000): 17–43.

31. McDermott, *Working-Class White,* 149.

The first finding of McDermott's study is the place of local context on white working-class identity and the meanings attached to it. She found a basic difference between the white working-class people in the Boston and the Atlanta neighborhoods. Although these two neighborhoods matched up similarly in the demographic profiles of US Census data, there were significant differences in the way whites saw themselves in the two city neighborhoods. She specifically points to factors such as the power of labor unions and the high rates of European ethnic immigration, which characterized the history of Boston but were not nearly as prominent in Atlanta. A powerful union presence can strengthen status claims, and pride in being Irish or Italian or Greek, for example, offer place in the world and can be sources of honor and legitimate standing. The neighborhood in Atlanta was quite otherwise in both these regards. They had "no sense of working class or ethnic solidarity." Further, they were conscious of how others saw them as "individual failures." They lived on the wrong side of town, close to a black residential area, so that these white working-class people keenly felt they "had failed to live up to expectations." In Boston, however, to be white was to be a person of "power and privilege," even if that did not translate into financial success.[32]

Second, McDermott says, "None of the 'white racists' that I grew to know were unambiguously bad people; all of them could be thoughtful, generous, and considerate" and almost always kind to children. In their racist expressions they were typically "reacting to the situations and circumstances in which they were embedded." She claims that race has been such a persistent and pervasive social influence that it has become "the filter" by which these working-class whites evaluated and judged the "rudeness, criminal intent, toughness, even lewdness" they encountered in and around the convenience stores.

At the same time, in the two stores, cordial and courteous encounters between black and white were so much the usual norm that race did not even seem to be an issue. But this congenial atmosphere could turn on a dime when a perceived slight or a loud, misunderstood expression could initiate a rude confrontation. These moments triggered anti-black

32. Ibid., 150.

or anti-immigrant sentiment. In these times, McDermott found "a free-floating prejudice" that seemed to encompass the ordinary, everyday interactions of people.[33]

Third, McDermott calls attention to the ways in which whites and blacks can misinterpret the intent of the other. While sometimes there is racist intent, other times there is not; but when not, misinterpretations can still build a wall of hostility between blacks and whites that is difficult to cross. Occasions such as these can generate "explosive situations" and can be quite alienating. McDermott's point is that misinterpretation of intent is a serious problem, one that requires its own kind of attention.[34]

Fourth, McDermott did not find among whites "evidence of a politically principled stance" with regard to racial questions; in other words, they did not approach particular political issues by drawing on "abstract principles of fairness, morality, or individualism." Rather, they wrapped political issues in racial terms; it was "the sense of being white—not of being American, or hardworking, or Republican—that drove the opinions of the working-class people" of her research. McDermott surmises that the reason for this dynamic was the high number of interracial contacts and encounters that occurred every day and made these whites more sensitive to racial identity. This identity held up on political issues, even though McDermott found that a "communitarian ethic . . . rather than an individualist one" typically spurred the convictions and practices of working-class whites in the neighborhoods of both Boston and Atlanta.[35]

Fifth, McDermott draws a connection between her findings on white racial identity and the research conducted on group threat. Here, again, she found an important difference between the neighborhood in Atlanta and the one in Boston. In the latter, she found "a clear sense of group threat," especially around jobs and housing, a finding growing out of "the situational context and the tenor of anti-black attitudes." In contrast, in the Atlanta neighborhood, where many whites felt like failures who had not lived up to expectations, the threat was more like a status threat—a

---

33. Ibid., 151.

34. Ibid., 152.

35. Ibid., 153.

reflection of the shame they felt in who they were and the limits of what they had accomplished.[36]

As have our other researchers, McDermott records a sixth finding that is desperately important to our work here: namely, "a backdrop of considerable stress and struggle," which characterizes the lives of these white working-class people as they encounter African Americans and racial tensions. The impact of class does indeed have its effects in worries about money, and the damage to self-esteem, that come with low status, low wages, and service work. In these white working-class communities there is ever the threat of crime and the constant pressure of urban living in lower class neighborhoods with "the lack of recreational space, and the general crush of traffic, pollution, noise, lousy schools, and limited opportunities." And, maybe, the worst comes with hidden injuries to self-respect that inevitably result from being white working-class in a society where meritocracy takes on such singular importance. McDermott found that even among the toughest of those she got to know there resided "a well of doubt and fatalism."[37]

McDermott, of course, does not forget in these comments the devastation of racism for African Americans, and I would say the last thing we need is a contest where energy is exhausted in arguing the damage each has experienced. We have more than enough problems to go around; what we need are the kinds of political moves, coalitions, and organizations of citizens that can take on the depredation and plunder of race and class, and certainly those of gender, orientation, and the other reigning structures of the kingdom of evil.

To sum up, we identified six significant learnings from McDermott's research that will enable us to address the issue of racism among white working-class people. Once again, we find the centrality of identity and the way it varies by context. Here again, class consciousness is not one thing. She identifies situations and circumstances that can trigger racist reaction, suggesting "a free-floating prejudice," that is quite ready, it seems, to take advantage of these moments, especially when there are

36. Ibid., 153–54.
37. Ibid., 155.

misinterpretations of intent. Further, "a sense of whiteness" played a more important role than did a given political position for the white working people McDermott studied. So, once again, we see how preponderant identity is in understanding politics and no few other issues. Finally, it is important on the basis of McDermott's research to distinguish group threat and status threat. Being able to diagnose which of these is at work in a repertoire of cultural resources, à la Lamont, is crucial not only to explore and determine what is going on in a given community but to make specific moves that address significant issues at hand.

Summary and Conclusion

This chapter began by drawing distinctions between prejudice and racism, especially the systemic and structural character of the latter. We used this distinction to question—no, really, to attack—the scapegoating of white working-class people. We offered an important study of Ferguson, Missouri as a microcosm of America, demonstrating the profound complicity of government, business, banks, and others that figure much more prominently in systemic and structural racism. To scapegoat white working-class people and to ignore the role of government, business, financial elites and their minions is to be engaged in mindless racist complicity.

We also looked back at the work of W. E. B. Du Bois and W. J. Cash for compelling analyses of the racism of white workers of yesterday. Du Bois made the historically important observation of "the wages of whiteness," the psychological payoffs and low-grade "privileges" gained by whites by not being black or slaves. Cash addresses the psychological compensative character of racism among white working-class people and the status they drew from that standing. These compensative dynamics identified by Du-Bois and Cash are important; they have certainly played a salient role in white working-class racism and should not be ignored.

We then turned to six important studies of white working-class people to explore more recent research on the racist dynamics at work in the hope that these analyses would provide current diagnoses from which more effective avenues for action might be determined. As it turns out, we did discover different expressions of racism and greater clarity and nuance about different forms it takes, forms that diverge in important ways from the psychologically compensative findings of DuBois and Cash.

To drive home the point again, with the work of Lamont, we are reminded of the important role of morality and the boundary work it does in making status distinctions among racial groups, especially in determining "us" and "them"; and, further, that racism is addressed more within the white working class's general moral worldviews, like patriotism, than through racism per se. With Gest, the powerlessness and marginality experienced by white working-class people, along with their perceptions that the historically disadvantaged are provided unfair opportunities, combine as factors to induce people into extremist groups like the Tea Party. Here, racism seems to provide no "wages"; it offers no psychological benefits; it is a resentment of being impotent and displaced. Meanwhile, Hochschild found the Tea Partiers she studied were shaped by a deep story about people who unfairly break in the line leading to the American Dream. Here, again, whiteness is not seen as a psychological benefit or asset, and the Tea Partiers perceive themselves as victims, or at least as people not receiving their due, standing in a long line that does not move.

In contrast, Sherman's work found hardly any racist references in her entire research. We learn from her, however, that traditional commitments, family rhetoric, and territorial location can offer legitimation and direction for adaptive and transformative change, a finding that provides a valuable avenue for social action. Similar to Sherman, Cramer found not a single racist reference in her meetings in small-town and rural Wisconsin. Instead, she found a rural consciousness in her subjects who felt disrespected, powerless, overtaxed, and underserved by government and other public institutions. Their resentment, however, was not aimed at people of color but at teachers, professors, public employees, and denizens of Madison and Milwaukee. Finally, McDermott contrasts the status threat experienced by white working-class people in Atlanta and group status threats by those in Boston, with quite different effects for both. In Atlanta the whites in the community she studied regarded themselves as failures who had not lived up to their own expectations of achievement. In this connection McDermott distinguishes group threat from status threat. In Boston white working-class people experienced group threats around jobs and housing, but in Atlanta the white working people she met felt shame over who they were and the little they had been able to attain.

Once again, the dynamics found in these studies are not like those of "the wages of whiteness." We face today more complicated forms of racism. It becomes very important diagnostically and therefore strategically to know which forms are operative in a given community. Moreover, it is not necessary to claim that the wages of whiteness no longer operate across the country, but it becomes rather just one of the types that require white working-class people, community workers, clergy, agency staff, and others to be alert to a range of racist forms and to be able to respond to these directly.

In the next chapter we turn to the matter of what is to be done not only about the prevalence of racism across the country but also with how we do social change with white working-class people. We will deal explicitly with a basic approach to social change with white working-class people. By working with these approaches, we will address specific avenues of action for resisting racism. In these strategies our focus will be on the granular practices of identifying with and working together with white working people in doing change.

CHAPTER 6

WHAT TO DO:
WORK INDIGENOUSLY

The last forty-five years have been hard times for the white working class. This deepening destitution requires significant strategies that are sensitive to the identity, dignity, moralities, approaches to life, ways of thinking, culture, and practices of working-class life. In other words, approaches to social change must be indigenous—again, in the good sense—to working-class life. We who usually teach must instead expect to learn. We who make our living giving our opinion must rather seek theirs. We who are typically competent in the skills associated with our profession must now move into an apprenticeship in the know-how, the craft, and the savvy of working-class life.

Again, this is not to suggest an uncritical approach to working-class life, neither is it to recommend that relating to white working people is a time to "go native" in some uninformed, awkward imitation and simply accommodate the practices that are there, whatever they are. Given the right direction, utilizing indigenous practices, and engaging working-class people with respect, there are ways to respond to their anger and pain through grassroots organizations and movements that offer a new direction.

Let me suggest some guidelines for working with white working-class people. Basic to these guidelines is the use of practices that are indigenous to the white working class and that take with the utmost seriousness the barrel of cultural resources it offers. These guidelines are not absolutes, but they really are *guidelines*, meant to suggest primary findings from the research we have considered. There are variations in the white working class, and attention must be sensitively given to the dynamics of a particular community in which one works.

Listening

First, those of us who talk for a living must especially learn to listen. If there is anything that comes through the research on white working class people, it is that they are the forgotten, ignored, disrespected, stereotyped, dismissed, denigrated, and, yes, the despised of our land. So far as I can tell, there is no other way into that morass of slander and neglect than listening, really listening. It does not begin with diagnoses of their false consciousness, their failures to follow their self-interest, their bad faith, and their hegemonic commitments; it is listening to learn the logics of their thinking, the tacit meanings "behind" their rhetoric, and the ways they name and deal with social wrongs.

REVEREND EMANUEL CLEAVER, II

The Rev. Emanuel Cleaver II is the congressional representative for the Fifth District of Missouri, where he has served since 2005. His district is clearly gerrymandered by the Republican Party, which has been in power throughout his congressional tenure. An African American, Cleaver's district encompasses the southern three-quarters of Kansas City, Missouri, but it also includes the largely rural counties of Lafayette, Ray, and Saline, to the east of the metropolitan area. The Republican Party typically wins big in rural Missouri, and these rural counties were included in Cleaver's district by the oppositional party in order to give advantage to Republican candidates.

Cleaver's main electoral strength resides in the black community that is located within municipal Kansas City. Yet Cleaver continues to be reelected in great part because of his commitment to listening and being present not only in the communities where he has political strength but in these rural counties as well. If anything happens in these small towns or open country settings, he appears. If there is a fire, a tornado, the closing of a school, or the death of a public figure or local luminary, he shows up and listens. One testimony to this came from a working-class white man during the 2016 campaign in which Cleaver was running for reelection. Cleaver was on the scene for Halloween and giving candy to children in one of the small towns of his district, when this white working-class man walked up to him and said, "Congressman Cleaver, I want you to know that I am going to vote for Donald Trump." The man paused a moment for dramatic effect and then added, "and I am going to vote for you." This is the power of listening, paying attention, and showing up with white working-class Americans.[1]

Listening also requires learning the indigenous practices of a community of people. I think here of the ability to be alert to indigenous practices as common as cursing and as complex as mutual insults among friends. For example, I will never forget reading for the first time Joe Bageant's comment that "cussing is a form of punctuation to us [white working-class people]."[2] It clarified a practice that I had tried to understand for most of my life. I have wondered why some people use the "f-word" in virtually every sentence. After Bageant's comment, I realized it often functions as a period but other times as a comma, a colon, a semi-colon, and often as an exclamation point. For the first time, I gained a first step on deciphering working-class cussing. (Most white working-class people do not curse, they *cuss*.)

Now, I do understand that there is a real difference between a working person who makes an art of cussing and those who—when it comes to cussing—don't know the difference between a comma and a quotation mark. There can be incompetence in the white working class, even in one of the most central of its linguistic performances. Some people really ought not to cuss, not so much on moral grounds, but just because they aren't good at it. I have known some great cussers in my life; it requires high sentential aestheticism.

---

1. This is an account of a story that Congressman Cleaver personally shared with me, with permission to share with you.

2. Joe Bageant, *Deer Hunting with Jesus: Dispatches from America's Class War* (New York: Crown Publishers, 2007), 23.

That Barrel (or Bucket) of Cultural Tools

A strategy that works with the granular practices of working-class discourses and more material activities will address what Lamont calls "a repertoire of cultural resources," and I like to call, in more worker lingo, a storage shed or supply house or just a good old *barrel*. For some things, I like the word *bucket* even better. As we have discussed, barrel (or bucket) contains a host of stories, ideas, proverbs, images, and national narratives, and these constitute the resources to address dignity, worth, family life, politics, money matters—you name it—as working people deal with the ongoing challenges of their lives. Here, a few comments are in order in terms of working with this barrel or bucket of cultural resources.

The first job in dealing with this barrel of resources is to be alert to the way these resources are used in a given community. This means being conscious of the practices at work, identifying them, and gaining respect for their use and importance. It may help to remember how complex and sophisticated these uses are in this regard. I recommend a reading of Aaron Fox's *Real Country*, where he does a close anthropological examination of the uses of language, its relationship to country music, and the range of questions it addresses in that honky-tonk in Lockhart, Texas.

Just one example: Fox's discussion of imperfection and eccentricity in working-class talk, country music, and their sizing up of life is worth the price of the book. Fox claims that imperfection is a figure or metaphor "of almost sacred meaning in working-class life." It has its historical and experiential roots in "the explicitly sacred realm of Christian theology." Imperfection takes on a very important role because most of the people in his research understood themselves as Christians, and no few of them were raised in fundamentalist churches and families.[3]

Imperfection was a trait not only to be owned up to but actively cultivated in the honky-tonk. It took place alongside some specific eccentricity that a person might have, and both were "not only tolerated but carefully nurtured and curated."[4] Even when the imperfection became an impedi-

---

3. Ibid., 109.

4. Ibid., 111.

ment to social relationships in the bar, other laudable qualities could justify a kind of social reinstatement with the group. For example, some imperfection and eccentricity could be combined with yet some other quality, one that was highly valued and gave a redemptive spin to that particular person's overall character. Fox names explicitly an "aesthetics of eccentricity," which became a requirement for "working-class sociability." In this sense, the honky-tonk became populated with a "bunch of characters," and talk about these highly personalized, unique individuals in comparison with yet other groups of characters became intrinsic to the social life, country music, and verbal art in Texas working-class life.[5]

The use of concepts like these in the talk of working-class Texans is a significant building block of sociability. Indeed, organizing with working people involves building relationships and doing so with practices that offer sociability of an indigenous kind, illustrated by factors such as imperfection and eccentricity and their importance for "a bunch of characters." I have found, for example, that after you have built a relationship with many working people, one of the best ways to continue to bond and build friendships with them is a kind of "insulting" banter that accuses them of being "bad people." It is ironic banter in the sense that you say the opposite of what you mean, which, of course, needs to be understood. I will say that I keep my hand on my wallet when I'm around—say Ellen or Joe—as a way to indicate that I trust them a great deal. They in turn will say that you had better watch your daughter or girlfriend when that preacher (meaning me) is around. These are the kinds of things you say only to people you really like and trust—and who know that; otherwise you may have a fight on your hands.

A second job in working with this barrel of resources is to pay attention to context, especially to know where one resource is appropriate and another is not. Knowing which setting requires a story or a proverb and which does not require a kind of environmental intuition, a sensibility for which one needs—I'm sure, talent—but just as much or more so a certain upbringing or even "informal" apprenticeship training. And, of course, the use of humor can hardly be exaggerated, but knowing which

---

5. Ibid., 114.

expression of it to use and where to employ it, or not, are profoundly related to context.

Third, the matter of context raises the important question of timing. Using a resource in the right place and at the right time are crucial in working in a white working-class community. Being able to recognize that pregnant moment, when the time is right, is related to a larger sensibility of the range of practices and to the temporal ecology of ordinary life.

I remember being present with a group of white working-class men in my hometown of Brookhaven, Mississippi, a year or so after the high school had been racially integrated. I had graduated from high school there some years before, and my Millsaps College and Boston University training, and civil rights activity, had rendered me a person under suspicion, to say the least. The conversation in the room turned rather abruptly into the integration of the high school, and I began to think of a way to intervene should the conversation turn racist, knowing full well that any such move on my part would be neither appreciated nor helpful.

In the group, however, was an uncle of mine who was as able a storyteller and humorist as I have ever known. I have seen him literally "entertain" groups of people for thirty minutes or longer simply by telling stories and jokes. His dialect and idiom were distinctly Mississippian and working class. Also, as it happened, that year the high school had a good football team, and clearly the best player was a very fast running back who was black. My uncle, in his usual deeply inflected Southern accent said, "You know, about the school, we got a damn good football team this year. I was at the game the other night, and we got this kid that's an Indian playing running back. He broke for a sixty-five-yard touchdown, and I just jumped up and started shouting, 'Look at that Indian go.'" The entire group collapsed in laughter, and the conversation switched to the football team and the season underway.

All the men in that room knew that the high school running back was not a Native American. Everyone in that room also loved football and supported the high school team to the hilt. Those men knew that without that running back the team did not stand a chance of winning the state championship. And each of them wanted that running back to continue to play football for Brookhaven High School. To place that is-sue in the "falsified" humorous framework that my uncle did was sheer genius. Out of the entire range of issues surrounding racial integration, my uncle picked the single most favorable aspect of the school racial in-tegration process—in fact, it might have been the only positive argument for integration with those men in that particular group—and he used it to reverse the flow of the conversation.

Now, I doubt that my uncle's story will pass muster in terms of the political rectitude of most of my friends who share my left-wing commit-ments. And, to this day, I do not understand why my uncle told that story. It could be that he was pro-integration of schools, although I'm not sure of that. It could be that he just felt that further resistance to integration and continuing support for segregation were bad for the town. It could be that he was protecting me, knowing where I was on the issue and not wanting me to become the object of the group's wrath. But I cannot think of a single response to that group at that time in that context with that timing and that use of humor that could have been more helpful or appropriate. I apologize to African American and Native American friends who find my uncle's story offensive. At the same time, his comment had a positive effect on that group, countered the racist tensions in the room, and transformed one particular, granular practice.

Another important guideline in white communities is to begin, not by working on racism or some other issue that is not perceived by them as their concern, but by working on justice for the white working class itself, taking their issues of identity, dignity, respect, income, work, job conditions, and the hardship of their lives as first priority. The issue of class must not be ignored or become a peripheral concern, or simply the avenue to "con" them into addressing other people's interests. To focus initially on racism, white privilege, or white supremacy; or the glass ceil-ing confronted by upper middle-class women; or marriage equality for the LGBTQ community, will be seen as one more attempt to ignore their concerns—really—to ignore them and to continue what they have expe-rienced now for decades.

Remember the point made by Lamont that white workers do not approach racism or any other issue directly but rather address them from within their moral worldviews, especially about such things as the disciplined self, hard work, responsibility, and providing for and protecting their families. This point suggests that it is crucial to learn what is indigenous and to get in touch with the rhetoric, logic, and the barrel or barrels of cultural resources operative in a particular community.

In this connection, take seriously Cramer's findings on rural consciousness, especially the outrage over distributive injustice. There is a great deal of work to be done in rural and small-town communities. Basic to this work will be greater factual clarity about where the problems actually reside, but this cannot be done without the utmost conviction that rural America has just claims of the highest order.

Precisely here, we must not forget that commitments like tradition, family rhetoric, and location or place, play a central role in adaptive and transformative change. They are critical to the work of justice. Such commitments are the crucial points at which one begins not only to join white working-class people but to initiate and sustain virtually any kind of social change. I shall say more about this below.

Further, working class people engage the world with story; and narratives are the embodiment of their wisdom, great sources of their humor, and rich ways of understanding the world and dealing with its mystery. Even more, much of their use of language is of a tacit kind, suggesting a contrast with more representative language. That is, their tacit language, like their tacit knowing, does not attempt to state in the descriptive and conceptual terms of high literacy a given topic or question but rather uses the ostensible situation to convey what they mean. Most of the skills and jobs of the working-class world are not learned through classrooms and literate manuals but through apprenticeship training and through being shown: "Do it like this." The point is to learn the tacit powers of narrative and the masterful art of storytelling. It is perhaps the central and most compelling form of communication available in white working-class communities.[6]

---

6. In this section I am referencing my article, "Laughing at What I Love: Notes on White Working-Class America," *Reflections*, Yale University Divinity School, 2013, https://reflections.yale.edu/article/future-race/laughing-what-i-love-notes-white-working-class-america.

Very important is the question of how to use criticism, how to do critique. In approaching this matter, it is important to remember that working people do not process language the way that college graduates do. Proverbs, adages, and sayings populate their talk. They reject the formalities and niceties of more "sophisticated" discourse. They are suspicious of fine print, big words, and fancy language, having been hustled by people using words these ways many times, not to mention the ways they are demeaned by those who use language and talk as expressions of status.

The point is to pay attention to the indigenous ways working people do critique and go to school on the characteristics and shapes of this practice. Learn how to raise questions with events, policies, and so forth, using working-class formats and moves. Typically, story, proverb, metaphor, and largely tacit claims will be important ingredients in this practice. Use these, for example, to address the issue of racism.

The best form of critique with working-class people occurs in the use of story. Specifically, it is being able to out-narrate a given story that is detrimental and/or oppressive to their lives. By "out-narrate" I mean simply to tell a better story, a more compelling account. I think particularly of Hochschild's study of Lake Charles, which we reported above. Her investigative research of the petrochemical industry discovered that this industry has not delivered on the crucial matter of bringing permanent jobs to the community; that it has in fact been subsidized and incentivized by state funding and contributed significantly to Louisiana's burgeoning debt; that the pollution and contamination were even worse than some knew; and that the impact on the medical well-being of its people had become deadly. Each of these violations related to the petrochemical industry can be placed in stories and grouped in a much larger story. What is important here is not only the statistics and information but the people's use of narrative and descriptive form. I've heard it said, "It is difficult to argue with a story," but working-class criticism embodied in an indigenous narrative is especially compelling. At the same time, the storytelling will need to be accompanied by the logics of the relationship thinking and the family rhetoric of working-class life, which we turn to next.[7]

---

7. One of the best sources of stories about the violations of corporate America and the Congress is Elizabeth Warren, *This Fight Is Our Fight: The Battle to Save America's Middle Class* (New York: Metropolitan Books, 2017).

Circles of Cooperating Kin

James Ault's study of a largely working-class, fundamentalist church outside Worcester, Massachusetts, found that white working people organize their lives in "circles of cooperating kin." He further argues that this "practical organization of life" characterizes working-class people and small, family-based businesspeople all across the country.[8] This kind of "popular conservatism," or "cultural traditionalism" (Levison), which Ault contends also has its "liberal counterpart," does not arise from specific religious or theological notions or traditions as such. This tradition—often called social conservatism, which basically generalizes and misses its dynamics—has to do with a range of discourses and practices that enable these families "to regulate, order and change family relationships, especially marriage." In the case of the fundamentalist church Ault studied, he found a "good fit between their habits of moral thought, cultivated in circles of relatives and family friends, on the one hand, and the theological and biblical discourses of this particular fundamentalist Baptist tradition, on the other."[9]

There is an intimate connection between the findings of Lamont and Sherman regarding the centrality of morality in the working people they studied and Ault's findings about a "popular conservatism" oriented around circles of cooperating kin. Lamont and Sherman rightly make a good deal of the boundary work being done by the moralities of the people they study. Their work underscores the kind of distinctions being made between the included and excluded in this morality. I do not argue with these results.

---

8. James M. Ault Jr., *Spirit and Flesh: Life in a Fundamentalist Baptist Church* (New York: Knopf, 2004), 204. Andrew Levison also discusses this pattern at length, which he calls "cultural traditionalism." He states that it is "essentially universal" in white working-class life. See Levison's book *The White Working Class Today: Who They Are, How They Think and How Progressives Can Regain Their Support* (Washington, DC: Democratic Strategist Press, 2013), 92.

9. Ault, *Spirit and Flesh*, 204–5.

FAMILIES, FRIENDS, AND "FAVORS"

My grandson, Blake, is a Teamster, but he has a community college degree in auto mechanics. Because of this skill he spends many weekends repairing the cars of family and friends, replacing brake linings, spark plugs, and various other auto parts. But his work on cars participates in a wide pattern of reciprocal "favors" in which he engages with buddies and kinfolk. His best friend, Adam, works in a battery factory and gets him special deals on batteries but also works with him on auto repairs as a favor. In return, Blake helps out with Adam's projects, and they work together on other ventures of common interest. Blake's mother gives Adam free haircuts because he will move furniture and other items for her in his big truck.

This reciprocation is not exactly a quid pro quo thing. It is not contractual clearly; it is also not quite covenantal. The former is too formal and the latter is a bit too exalted. It's more ordinary, like a way of life. Friends and family just do it for each other. It does, however, have serious and significant consequences. When money is short or not there, when life in general is hard or, at least, difficult, these favors not only help people cope and survive, but they also generate bonding, building relationships and community in neighborhoods and across neighborhoods in the midst of an otherwise pervasive urban anonymity.

When our house was burglarized, we arrived home just in time to scare the burglar away. Within thirty minutes every member of our extended family was at our house to help, including Adam...and his mother! We were fortunate that in his haste to get away the burglar hit a curb just a hundred yards from our home and blew out a tire on the stolen car he used. We recovered each of the stolen items, and by midnight Blake and Adam had every TV, computer, printer, electric appliance—everything—back in place and hooked up.

At the same time, I contend that a basic way to address the boundaries people construct, and even to change them, is by means of working through the logics of these extended family relationships identified by Ault. That is, to shift boundaries requires new ways of thinking about family relationships. I am reminded here of Sherman's finding that these moralities are not only adaptive but can also be transformative. As "flexible men" in Sherman's study began to think through the implications of Golden Valley's economic hardship for their wives, children, and

97

themselves, they shifted not only their behavior but the norms that govern those family relationships. In effect, the boundaries around the roles of men and women shifted as they reworked their lives together in the light of the severe financial and economic hardships they faced.

Lamont sees morality and boundary work as closely intertwined, and I do not argue with her findings. In terms of making social change, however, I would argue that the primary focus of change needs to be on these circles of family relationships more than attempts to address the patterns of inclusion and exclusion directly. That is, the legitimation of change will come from compelling arguments growing out of family relationships rather than explicit rhetoric oriented around race and the poor. By this comment, I do not mean to suggest that we do not address matters of race and poverty; but rather that we deal with them through the logics of these circles of family life.

To say this one more way, white working-class people think in terms of family and other primary relationships. The family is the core institution. They seek cooperation among key groups such as family, school, church, and other traditional institutions. Their political and economic positions on social issues are not at the base of the lives and practices of these working families. More foundational are the relationships, convictions, commitments, and practices that enable these families to deal with a world that does not come out right. This means that their political attitudes can vary significantly, depending on how a given question relates to their lives in these terms.

The great majority of white working-class families do not listen to the National Organization of Women or Focus on the Family. They do not turn to Fox Fictional News or the Ku Klux Klan, not even the American Legion and the National Rifle Association; though, of course, these influence some. They are far more likely to tackle problems by thinking about them in terms of how they affect their families, the cooperative institutions upon which they depend, and the morality that sustains the structure of these relationships and enables them to manage and to make it through the night.

Thus, a significant resource is the use of rhetoric growing out of these reciprocating family relationships. From here on I will refer to this simply as *family rhetoric*. Addressing racism, for example, down on the ground with white working people, involves having a compelling set of stories of black families and what they do, how they struggle, and, particularly, some of the commonalities they share with white working people in terms of hard times. These stories are not to be used primarily to privilege black or white narratives, but to communicate common circumstances and build a common ground. I have seen this work so many times in community organizing when we have blacks and whites and browns stand up and tell stories of their families, of working more than one job, of doing their dead level best to be good providers and to take care of their families. These are hard-core narratives, and they can have surgical impact in cutting away certain images of inclusion and exclusion.

Identity, Tradition, and Place

There can hardly be a question about the importance of the role of identity in white working-class life. Gaining a sense of who one is through hard work, responsibility, protection of and providing for the family, being a good American, fulfilling the American Dream, being patriotic, serving in the military—and, for some—being a Christian: these are among the most important ingredients in the determination of working class identity. They are sources of personal worth and honor. These ingredients can compensate for the lack of material success and counter the slights, the pain, and the damages from the hidden injuries of class.

In our time when there have been so many assaults on working-class unions, good jobs, living wages, pension programs, and the dismissal and neglect of white working-class people, even by progressives, identity becomes a matter of desperate proportions. We have already heard about many white working-class voters who vote on the basis of their identity more than on some estimation of their self-interest and people who see the haves in terms of culture rather than of wealth. All of these speak to the central importance of identity among the working class.

Appeals to identity become a strategic necessity in times like these. To neglect this issue or to dismiss or demean it, as so many on the left have done, is a blunder of historic proportions. The mobilization and organizing of white working-class people require specific reference to their identities and direct attention to their plight and their hopes. Any electoral coalition of the so-called new demographics that the Democrats are so wont to speak of will finally fail, if it does not include this very large contingent of people in our society. We have seen this play out rather persistently across the last forty-five years. The impact of identity in the mobilization of white working-class people can only be enhanced when combined with traditional values and overtures to the importance of place.

Both Sherman and Cramer in their research identified the importance of tradition and place and demonstrated the ways these are interlaced. From Alasdair MacIntyre we learn that tradition is a contested, and certainly not an unchanging, social process. Moreover, anthropologist Talal Asad contends that tradition is very much embodied in practices and performance. It is not something simply in one's head or one's assertions and arguments. It is exercised. It involves certain disciplines and is attentive to authorities and to people who master its practices.[10]

It is important to see tradition operating this way in working-class life. The host of practices, for example, around traditional family life involves actions and performances. I think of practices of affection, cooking and house upkeep, auto repair, the care and oversight of children, meals together, celebrations and festivities, the rush of getting people off to work and children off to school, and paying bills and managing debt. I also think of people who are master practitioners in these activities and to whom working people turn for wisdom and direction, such as grandparents, especially grandmothers, as well as uncles and aunts, family members, and close friends who have excelled at or are recognized for wisdom along the lines of some endeavor.

The importance of place in a tradition takes on a gravity of its own. The love of Golden Valley, as found in Sherman's research, and the identifications with the small cities and rural areas of Wisconsin in Cramer's study both speak to a territorial rootedness for many in working-class life. Also,

---

10. Charles Hirschkind and David Scott, eds., *Powers of the Secular Modern: Talal Asad and His Interlocutors* (Stanford, CA: Stanford University Press), 234–35.

the significance that an urban neighborhood in a metropolitan area can have must not be forgotten. My focus here, however, is the role that place can play in social change, especially in providing legitimation for organizing and action. I think particularly of the way that traditional commitments, especially around the family, and around place, can drive mobilizing efforts.

For example, I am amazed at the radical difference between a fundamentalist, free-market capitalism and traditional family commitments of working-class people. A powerful use could be made of these traditional family commitments to counter the market ideology of right-wing political efforts. Notice that the laissez-faire, right-wing focus is on the free individual, who is "prior" to society and the state. This individual pursues self-interest in a competitive free market. The conviction is that individualistic pursuit of self-interest in a free market results in the greatest good of the greatest number. Defenders of this position support high military spending in a minimalist state, and their greatest fear is the loss of market freedom.

In sharp contrast, traditional working-class people place primary emphasis on the family, not the free individual. They do not stress self-interest, especially of an individualistic kind, because it is corrosive of family relationships. This is especially so in the case of the man, provided there is one, as the primary breadwinner. If he pursues his individual self-interest, he may walk out the door, leaving his poor family devastated or near-poor family poverty-stricken. Further, the greatest fear of these families is moral corruption and this for a basic reason. Ault makes the case that morality in this culture serves to support the structure of family relationships in order to cope and survive. Further, he finds that this kind of traditional culture basically operates to control male sociality and minimize the potentially disruptive behavior of men in these settings.[11] These commitments by

---

11. Ibid., 189–200. Country music is filled with songs about men who walk out the door and the devastation it brings. Or, see songs like "Good Hearted Woman," who is "in love with a good timing man," or "Mamas, Don't Let Your Babies Grow Up to Be Cowboys." Let me clarify at this point, too, that I am describing here especially a very large group of white working-class people often described as "respectables" or "settled living." My comments here would require more nuance if the focus were on those called "hard living." See Joseph T. Howell, *Hard Living on Clay Street: Portraits of Blue-Collar Families* (New York: Anchor Books, 1973). See also my book *Hard Living People and Mainstream Christians* (Nashville: Abingdon Press, 1993).

working-class people stand in polar contrast to the free market ideology; and identity, traditional values, and place have the power to legitimize social action.

Someone may object that these kinds of working-class commitments simply fly in the face of liberative efforts like those of the LGBTQ movement. I thoroughly disagree. First of all, I have never seen a social issue that has had such success in so relatively short a time. I joined the LGBTQ movement in the late 1960s; I could not have then dreamed in my wildest imagination that they would have experienced such acceptance by the American people, even though, yes, we still have a long way to go. Also, I have been in dozens, maybe hundreds, of conversations with white working-class people about this issue. Over and over again, I have experienced the power of talking about gay and lesbian people they knew in their families or their friend's families who lived in their neighborhood or community. The matter of welcoming gay and lesbian people quite simply changes when you are talking about Fred or Jane, gay and lesbian respectively, who are the children of Max and Ethel and live in Every Town, USA. In fact, I don't know of any, not one, strategy even so nearly effective with white working-class people. Why can we not learn this politically?

Regarding racism, I have been intrigued by biracial marriages among the white working-class relationships I have. I think particularly of the way that talk about one young black man, who married a white woman, in a white family focuses on the fact that he makes good money, he works hard, he is a good provider, and he affords the opportunity for his wife to pursue further education. Yes, a few people in her extended family continue to disapprove, but the great majority clearly has accepted him and has done so through the legitimation of a *family rhetoric*. I know this is a small step, but it is happening across this country, and these examples provide opportunity to work on stereotypes and to break down walls of exclusion.

Categories and Vocabularies

There is yet one final pair of issues to discuss regarding white working-class people, two issues that certainly deserve strategic consideration. I am thinking here of the categories and vocabularies housed in the barrel of cultural resources and, also, of new ingredients to be placed there. Talal Asad argues that we live in fields of categories (and certainly we do), and they constitute no little space in that white working-class barrel.[12] As with any store of cultural resources there are categories that harm, promote the concepts of the dominating order, hold people captive, distort and obscure the actual lives of real people, and conceal the robbery and malfeasance of corporate criminality.

WHITE TRASH TALKING?

In 1986 Matthew Mickler published *White Trash Cooking* (Berkeley, CA: Ten Speed Press), which sold a half million copies with great success among white middle-class readers. Upon examination, however, Dina Smith found that many of the recipes in the book came from Junior League members and the author's middle-class kin. What is not to be found, of course, is any suggestion of problems with "white trash" labeling, or the impact of the postindustrial economy and its obsolescence-wielding power, that turns literally millions of people into relics. Nothing in the book offers a material look at the burdening oppression of poverty. Rather, poverty becomes "a quaint culture" with the book offering a false nostalgia.[13]

Unfortunately for Mickler, on the cover of the book he placed the picture of a Mrs. Ledbetter, a rural woman who sold watermelons. In the picture she sits upon a ripped chair, on a beat-up porch, wearing a threadbare dress, and offering watermelons for a dollar a piece. What never gets attention in this book is how someone like Mrs. Ledbetter makes a living in a postindustrial economy selling watermelons for such a low price. Yes, she harks back to an earlier, supposedly less harsh, time, but one wonders, for whom? Certainly not Mrs. Ledbetter. Her picture and *White Trash Cooking* are commodities; her life and her struggles are romanticized, commodified, and obscured.

---

12. Talal Asad, *Genealogies of Religion* (Baltimore: Johns Hopkins University Press, 2009). See his discussion of the power of vocabularies, 43–54.

13. Dina Smith, "Cultural Studies' Misfit: White Trash Studies," *Mississippi Quarterly* LVII, no. 3 (Summer 2004): 376–79.

Mrs. Ledbetter, however, did not appreciate being identified with the label "white trash." She also resented the fact that the author did not ask for permission to use her picture. So, she sued him and his publisher and was awarded $60,000. Dina Smith comments that this amount of money probably went mostly to Mrs. Ledbetter's attorneys; nevertheless, it amounted roughly to the royalties for the first year's sales of the book.

Smith maintains that as the economy continues to change we will see a generation of new "trash populations." They are "part of the social and cultural logic of an ever-shifting capitalism. " Today, commitment to high mobility with its resulting obsolescence for so many seems to be the destiny of our economy for the foreseeable future. Smith observes that in a service-oriented economy, class alignments are connected with lifestyle choices. She suggests that now "the marker of class privilege is no longer how much you consume (the high-industrial model) but rather how many consuming identities you can perform."[14]

Central to her argument is the circumstance that the more one is privileged, the more one can take on "white trash" identities without, of course, participating in the economic realities of the white working-class poor. Reading Smith's writing makes the posturing of a white trash identity by affluent people seem like a variant of Halloween. The rubberized monster headgear and the cheap gauze costumes convey a comical representation, but they can be removed conveniently and stored until they are needed again. Meanwhile, one does not have to live the life of monster, ghoul, or ghost.

Smith's work is an indictment on those who use labels like "white trash" and "redneck" that erase the down to earth, ordinary lives of the working class and working-class poor. Smith's essay points out what we must not do, but she also calls us to be alert to the changing usages of denigrative concepts like "white trash" and "redneck" and the functions they perform in our economy, especially the consumerist functions they presently fulfill. In her account she identifies a basic contradiction: what seems to be the privileging of "white trash" actually conceals working-class lives and turns the suffering of their hardship—and, for many, poverty—into a quaint nostalgia. Anthony Giddens, the British sociologist, states that it is more important to understand the contradictions a culture enacts than the functions it fulfills.[15] This is certainly the case in the social dynamics identified by Smith.

---

14. Ibid., 386.

15. Anhony Giddens, *Central Problems in Social Theory: Action, Structure, and Contradiction in Social Analysis* (Berkeley: University of California Press, 1979), 131–64, especially 131.

Of course, there are many categories often associated with the white working-class economy like "welfare queen," the so-called right to work, free enterprise, "corporations as persons," "money as free speech," "the undeserving poor," "the culture of poverty," "redneck," and a host of racial epithets, among others. Any and all of these categories can reside in that barrel of cultural usage of the white working class. For instance, I was told by a statewide labor leader that half of his union members would vote for the "right to work" if given the opportunity. Yet, the so-called right to work has been one of those conservative efforts that has contributed greatly to the weakening of organized labor over the past forty-five years. There is no question that the flattening and/or decline of worker's wages are decidedly influenced by these legislative and policy moves.

I have already used one word that needs to become a part of that barrel of cultural resources for white working-class people: *wealthfare*. In chapter 1 (page 13) I reported two studies about Walmart; one revealed it has received government subsidies in excess of $14 billion.[16] In the Kansas City newspaper there was an article in which city officials in Raytown, Missouri, accused the local Walmart store of "bleeding this town." Raytown is a municipality of the Metropolitan Kansas City Missouri/Kansas complex, and a large number of hardworking wage earners live there.[17]

The problem is that the local Raytown police made more than five hundred arrests at Walmart last year; the store is the site of 30 percent of the city's reported serious crimes. Yet Walmart pays no taxes that support law enforcement services. When the store was built, Walmart received a tax incentive finance deal that "diverts" about $300,000 in potential tax revenue away from public safety every year. Because of financial pressures Raytown cut budgets across all city departments. The police department alone lost thirty jobs, which include officers, civilians, and detectives.[18]

Walmart's response was that it hires off-duty officers for security on their premises. But city police must still come to the store to make arrests

---

16. David Cay Johnston, *Free Lunch: How the Wealthiest Americans Enrich Themselves at Government Expense and Stick You with the Bill* (New York: Penguin Books, 2007), 13, 100.

17. Ian Cummings, "Walmart's Bleeding This Town, Raytown Official Says," *Kansas City Star*, September 28, 2017, 6A.

18. Ibid.

even if security personnel detain shoplifters. So, if they are making more than five hundred arrests per year, local police are likely making more than forty arrests a month at the local Walmart store, for which Walmart pays nothing in taxes. "Walmart has defended its security policies, saying that if its store generates a lot of police calls, it is because the company is catching a lot of criminals."[19] In a later editorial the sarcastic response of *The Star's* editors is, "Gosh, so civic minded."

In the same editorial, *The Kansas City Star* states directly that public officials should not give out tax incentives "as if they were Halloween candy, to anyone who shows up at the door in plastic fangs or a sparkly tiara." The editors ask the pointed question of why a company that average $15.5 billion in annual profits over the past five years "ever needed or deserved a tax break."[20]

The Star editorial goes on to observe that while Walmart sidesteps its "fair share of taxes," taxpayers "subsidize the services needed by those thousands of the Arkansas company's low paid employees who are on public assistance." One alderman wants Walmart declared "a public nuisance"—a creative use of vocabulary and conceptualization—so that the city can bill the store for public services.[21]

The paper's editors remind local readers that the original purpose of tax incentive financing was to enable development projects that would not otherwise occur in "economically struggling areas." But this original purpose of the TIF has been diverted into support for America's big corporate businesses and to already profitable local enterprises.

This is precisely the kind of story that must be told over and over again in the white working-class world, and the category of "wealthfare" must be attached to it repeatedly. I remember an old saying, "If you want the water to be clean, you gotta get the hogs out of the creek upstream."

We need a profusion of concepts with appropriate vocabulary to characterize what is happening to working people; indeed, to the overwhelming

---

19. Ibid.

20. "To Get a Crime-Ridden Walmart, Raytown Gave Away the Store," editorial, *The Kansas City Star*, September 29, 2017, 12A.

21. Ibid.

majority of the American people. We especially need concepts and vocabularies that will appeal to the "tell it like it is" style of working-class talk. I think of words like "plutocrat" and "oligarch" to characterize corporate leadership, or "the tyranny of corporate globalization," or "corporate empires." Concepts like "crime scene" could better characterize the closing down of highly profitable industries and businesses in the United States when they move to other countries. The takeover and disembowelment of some American industries could be called "manufacturing murder." Further, I think it is probably appropriate to call most of our Senate and Congressional members "gigolos" and "prostitutes," because they basically sell their bodies and souls to corporate America. This is also true in many state legislatures. In Missouri there is no limit on campaign contributions that can be made to those running for public office. A member of the Kansas City Worker Rights Board reports that a Missouri state legislator told him emphatically, "I do not care what my constituents think." In other words, he's bought by other interests. Finally, "Koch Congress" or better a "Congress on Koch" is another favorite label of mine, but I think next to *wealthfare*, I prefer "legal criminality" or maybe just the word "brothel"—so long as we remember that most of the professionals "servicing" corporate America are men.

Racism

Finally, let me respond more specifically to the issue of racism. The issue of *wealthfare* applies directly to the issue of racism in the white working class. Discussing racism must not be avoided. The well-being of the white working class *and* people of color depends on attacking and changing the patterns of racism in our country. We cannot address the realities of class without dealing with those of race. Racism and classism are so profoundly intertwined that neither one can exclude the other. Yet strategies of "divide and conquer" by power elites have split the working class— white Americans and people of color. Indeed, sometimes the powerful split people of color between its diverse racial groups.

So, first, let me say that an approach to racism with respect to the white working class will involve a sensitivity to the current desperation of white working-class lives. It will involve the building of trust through listening and drawing on the barrel of cultural resources outlined above. It means thinking relationally through the circles of cooperating kin; it involves drawing on the cultural resources of identity, tradition, and place; and it will require a reconstruction of categories and vocabularies, as I have suggested.

Further, there are specific avenues for anti-racist work that grow from our review of research. I will repeat a few comments from the above not only for emphasis but to underline their importance for working on racism as well. The first of these is to remember again that identity and worldview profoundly determine white working-class politics. It is not the other way around. For example, harping on self-interest that ignores identity and worldview is futile activity. Moreover, in this worldview, morality is key and represents a powerful social force by which white working-class life is ordered. This ordering relates to survival, coping in their world, and attempting to make it through the hard times. Dealing effectively with racism will require addressing these issues of identity and worldview.

Furthermore, at the center of the difficulty of white working-class racism is the interlaced character of morality and the dynamics of distinction that drive racist principles of inclusion and exclusion. This means that new forms of identity are required. These new identities cannot ignore the rightful claims of working-class people to sustain their families, get decent work, make a living wage, and flourish. The good news is that this new identity is to be built on many laudable working-class practices already in place, both linguistic and material, that are to be respected, even honored. That is, this work does not have to start from scratch.

At the same time, there are changes to be made in who gets identified as *us* and who is defined negatively as *them*. We need an identification of *them* as the powers that be: "the 1 percent"; corporate America; a sold-out Congress; and those who make laws, policies, and procedures that transgress against both people of color and the white working class. This suggests a host of new stories "telling it like it is" with the highly-etched characters of oral presentation that tells *tales*, names *names*, identifies *actions*, and provides new *vocabularies* and concepts. It needs to be understood that American capitalist greed is "an equal opportunity employer" without regard to class, race, gender, sexual orientation, age, disability, religion, or transgender identification. Exploitative fornication is intrinsic to its being. It will screw over anybody.

We have mentioned national narratives such as Manifest Destiny, American exceptionalism, and the American Dream. In the history of the United States these narratives have often been intertwined with racism, and they require careful critique. They need to be reconstrued—and in some cases, rejected outright. Such criticism can only be done by those who are deeply trusted and on the basis of other commitments and convictions that have more final and ultimate claims.

According to the research we reviewed, it is not generally effective to employ arguments based on *multiculturalism* and *diversity*. Rather, use those that suggest the commonality of all people, the lineage that everyone shares, and make it clear that every race has both good and bad people. These are far more compelling and do not suggest the kind of relativism and potential disruption to the strength of a moral order required for white working families to stay together and make it through hard times.

An assessment of the nature of the threat, as reported by McDermott and as perceived by white working-class people, is necessary. A response to group threat will be quite different from that of a status threat. Both of these involve careful listening, but in the former it will require sharp clarification of the situation, interracial organizing, and the delineation of next steps to deal with, for example, jobs and housing. Networking and the engagement of local government, businesses, unions, and coalitions of action groups are among the first steps. In the latter, attention must be given to the dynamics around status. To deal with the wages of whiteness is one thing; to relate to people feeling deprived, fatalistic, defeated, powerless, and demoted to the edges of community life is another. Building relationships with people of color, bonding people together, participating in a welcoming church, getting people out of isolation, and providing hope are important dimensions of any effective response.

In some communities, racism may not be a major issue; rather, for example, it may be the issue of economic devastation as in Golden Valley or that of the rural disadvantage as in the small towns and open country of Wisconsin. This does not mean that racism doesn't exist, but there may be important opportunities for rural and urban coalitions to work on problems of common concern. In fact, such coalitions are much needed, and innovative work in this area could bring important results. We shall turn to these in the next chapter.

Summary and Conclusion

To summarize and conclude, I suggest engaging in social change through legitimate, granular practices of an indigenous approach to white working-class people. This involves the exploration of that *barrel* of cultural resources and tools employed in a community and giving explicit attention to the local practices at work there, being careful not to generalize practices across specific contexts and instead identify those at work in particular places.

I have underlined the importance of factors of sociability, timing, humor, and doing critique in line with local ways. Especially important are the circles of cooperating kin and thinking relationally of these circles when both analyzing a community problem and gaining legitimacy when taking a stand through social action.

Further, I have addressed the issue of concepts and the necessity, on the one hand, of working through vernacular vocabularies of a given community; while, on the other hand, introducing new ways to identify and call out dominating actions by oppressive power elites and corporations in these times of a rapacious capitalism.

Finally, using that vernacular *barrel* of cultural resources, and working with indigenous practices, we have named specific approaches to address racism with anti-racist practices that were identified in the research reported here. The combination of basic working-class practices and indigenous anti-racist arguments are intrinsic to battling racism in white working-class America.

I want to emphasize that systemic and structural realities of racism and classism will never be addressed adequately by the granular practices we have identified, when taken alone. Significant change will occur through broad-based, down-on-the-ground coalitions of working people—both white people and people of color—organized for community action. If we are to deal with the isolation of racial groups from one another, and the ignorance resulting from silos of race and class, the best hope is through the contact and bonding of working together in the struggle for justice and the common good. We turn to the importance of these subjects in the next chapter.

CHAPTER 7

WHAT TO DO: COMMUNITY ACTION

We turn now to strategies of community action to look at possible options for white working-class organizing and a few of the different fronts upon which this work can be done. We will examine both metropolitan and rural areas. The aim here is to look especially at coalition efforts because of the necessity of getting the white working class together with others to work for the common good. Coalition efforts are needed not simply for their strategic effectiveness but because they offer opportunities to break down the sense of isolation, neglect, and marginalization that so many working-class people experience.

Focus on Cities and City Hall, Not the White House

Significant change occurring in our cities offers opportunities for new efforts by community action groups. In this regard, sociologist Benjamin Barber challenges the division of American politics into blue and red states with "two multicultural liberal coasts flanking a homogenized heartland of rural/suburban conservatism." He claims instead that we have "a nationwide canvas of rural and exurban red, accented evenly right across the continent with swatches of blue." The latter are the cities that represent a far different political point of view than do those on the rural and exurban red landscape.[1]

The way forward through this political and economic morass, says Barber, is through the cities. He argues that community activists "need to focus less on who is in the White House and more on who is in City Hall." He believes that urban city councils are far more important than the Congress. The antidote for our snake-bitten political economy resides in the metropolis, where significant challenges can be made to "abusive-central government power."[2]

To start with, argues Barber, the US Constitution's Ninth and Tenth Amendments stand as checks on the authority of the president of United States and provide openings for community organizations working in cities across the country. Barber points out that 63 percent of our nation's population resides in its cities, a powerful and significant base not only for resistance to national power elites and concentrations of wealth but also as a center for social action and constructive change. Barber names New York and Chicago, for examples, the two cities where the fight for fifteen dollars an hour and a union began for low wage workers. Moreover, urban-based campaigns have led the fight for "paid-sick-leave legislation, fair-workweek initiatives, and universal pre-kindergarten programs." He reports further that twenty-five mayors and urban leaders started Cities for Action, a coalition to reach out to and support new immigrants. He further mentions sanctuary city efforts and other actions to protect immigrants.[3]

Barber makes trenchant claims that the old political parties, Democrat and Republican, no longer work and that the truly functional political entities are the cities. He asserts that "a fundamental devolution of power is underway"—beginning sometime before the rise of right-wing populism in both Europe and America—affirming that democratic sovereignty has its base in the people and thereby provides the legitimacy for

---

1. Benjamin Barber, "In the Age of Donald Trump, the Resistance Will Be Localized," *The Nation*, January 18, 2017, https://www.thenation.com/article/in-the-age-of-donald-trump-the-resistance-will-be-localized/.

2. Ibid.

3. Ibid.

"the vertical separation of powers." Basic to Barber's contention is support for the federalist principle laid out in the Ninth and Tenth amendments.[4] Barber believes that the voice of the city is now the voice of history, and that the Constitution provides the authority and powers for the cities to defend an inclusive, diverse, ecologically sustainable, and just new day.[5]

Let me say, that many of us who have seen abuse of local power across our lifetime—especially by those denying rights to people of color, women, immigrants, and others—have suspicions because of the miserable history of state's rights and the violations by municipalities and counties across this country. But Barber's argument for federalism by no means excludes the Bill of Rights and its guarantees to those very people at the bottom of the society from whom the sovereignty of the state derives. As always, the struggle for human dignity never ends, and the defense of human rights and bottom-up sovereignty will be with us for any foreseeable future.

Let me say, also, that Barber's voice is very much an urban one. His rhetoric and confidence in the blue cities will not go well in rural and small-town Wisconsin and with the rural consciousness Cramer discovered. Further, the rural-urban divide is not addressed by Barber's proposals; but in the previous chapter I discussed granular strategies and tactics appropriate to those settings, and I will return to those concerns again in chapter 8.

For now, I want to affirm Barber's urban strategy without making it the exclusive route to take. To do so, we will look at local examples of such a cities approach; but we will move outside the confines of the big

---

4. The Ninth Amendment states: "The enumeration in the Constitution, of certain rights, shall not be construed to deny or disparage others retained by the people," and the Tenth reads "the powers not delegated to the United States by the Constitution, nor prohibited by it to the States, are reserved to the States respectively, or to the people." "Constitution Annotated," https://www.congress.gov/constitution-annotated.

5. My support for the moral and strategic insight of Barber does not extend to some claims he makes about the cities that strike me as romantic. For example: "These blue clusters [on the red and blue political state maps] are blue cities, where people live because they believe in public goods, appreciate diversity, support creativity, and define their relationship to the interdependent planet in terms of cooperation rather than rivalry, networking rather than independence. They face forward, moving with history's winds at their backs. They recognize that globalization cannot be rolled back but must be democratized. They look to bridges, not walls, as instruments of accommodation." From Barber, "In the Age of Donald Trump."

metropolitan areas like New York, Los Angeles, Boston, and San Francisco. We will examine settings that are decidedly in the heartland. While I am glad for strategies and tactics hammered out in these coastal behemoths, we need models from the so-called flyover cities and rural America so often dismissed by "social justice elites" who reside in the metropolitan grandeur of oceanfront "cosmopolitanism."

The White Working Class of the Heartland of America

It seems clear that an important avenue of action is, indeed, in the urban centers of our country. I want to turn now, however, to the heartland of America, to the white working-class people there of metropolitan, rural, and small-town life. These working people pose a special predicament we have not yet adequately considered: that is, the fact that many of them hold views on social questions that stand in sharp discontinuity with the way they vote. Many of them are more open to change in their political and policy attitudes than they are in their electoral choices. This means, also, that when they respond to polls they support policies that seem to fly in the face of their electoral support of right-wing politicians. The work of Andrew Levison is the most sane and compelling account of this phenomenon I have seen. He names a number of factors that account for this seeming "contradiction."[6]

For one thing, he identifies partisan identity as more motivating and more determinative of their vote than their social attitudes as such. They

---

6. Andrew Levison, "Is There a Viable Progressive Strategy to Increase White Working-Class Support in the 'Conservative Heartland'?," *The Democratic Strategist*, 2017. http://thedemocraticstrategist-roundtables.com/is-there-a-viable-progressive-strategy-to-increase-white-working-class-support-in-the-conservative-heartland/. Levison also published a very important book in 2013 that still has sharp relevance for understanding the white working class. See *The White Working Class Today: Who They Are, How They Think and How Progressives Can Regain Their Support* (Washington, DC: Democratic Strategist Press, 2013). I use his article in this discussion primarily because it is more recent, but his book is a very important contribution to present day considerations, especially in providing more detail around a number of questions. It deserves a wide and careful reading. Note, too, that Levison is a consultant and strategist for the Democratic Party who is working for progressive causes. In the last chapter, I distinguish my view on behalf of the common good from that of a progressive position.

care more about their political party team and its winning an election than they do about a given issue. He states explicitly an observation that reverberates with findings we have already reported: people will vote their identities first and only then their policy commitments.[7]

Levison points out that this "disjunction" occurs across the nation, but it is especially evident in the heartland, by which he means the South, the Plains, and the Rocky Mountain states. In the South white racial attitudes are powerfully determinative, but in all three heartland areas a religious fundamentalism and an "anti-government consciousness" are at work. Levison names four salient value systems that are oriented around the church, the military, small business, and the school system, which in interaction support a religious piety, patriotism, free enterprise, and the American system of government. He contrasts this with the non-heartland states where the influences of strong unions, Democratic clubs, and liberal Roman Catholic Churches stand for a kind of New Deal liberalism.[8]

Yet in both of these conservative and liberal camps there is an "essentially universal respect for traditional institutions and culture" among working-class people that Levison calls "cultural traditionalism."[9] Even so there is a profound division between heartland white workers who are politically conservative and those who are more politically moderate to progressive. The more right-wing heartland voter tends to be rather intolerant; the heartland moderates and progressives tend to be tolerant and hold populist views about the economy.

There are, nonetheless, contradictions even within these more conservative *heartlanders*. There are those who take a hard-right view; for example, against gun control, and yet may be positive about immigrants coming into the United States. Levison clarifies that this does not mean that such folk have "a coherent group of consistently liberal or progressive" ideas. Rather, their views vary by issue and individual by individual.

Still, Levison acknowledges that it is difficult "to attack this entire complex of attitudes." He does claim, however, that ingredients of these

---

7. Ibid.

8. Levison, *The White Working Class Today*, 86.

9. Ibid., 92.

right-wing views can be "weakened" and "destabilized." Key to this effort is an accurate pinpointing of what he calls "the basic cognitive structure" of white working-class people and the pursuit of strategies that seek change from within that "framework."[10] His comment here is close to the approach we have advanced in this book. My only qualification is that the barrel of cultural elements is more encompassing than cognitive structure, at least if the latter is narrowly conceived.

Nevertheless, Levison suggests two basic approaches to this situation. The first is single-issue organizing that typically takes form around economic matters. The second is to work on a wide-ranging approach that takes on multiple issues through coalitions of community groups. To illustrate the first of these he calls attention to North Dakota, which voted no to a personhood amendment and at the same time elected a Republican to the House of Representatives. And Arkansas, Nebraska, and South Dakota voted in a Republican senator and governor and yet approved a minimum wage. Levison says that these traditionalist heartland workers will support a minimum wage increase, progressive taxes on the wealthy, keeping undocumented or "illegal" immigrants in the United States, efforts to stop global warming—even making same sex marriage lawful—and reforming the Affordable Care Act rather than its repeal![11]

Levison identifies conditions that seem to be operative among the white working class people who back single-issue efforts. Typically, these issues come in the form of community problems that surface quickly, issues such as toxic dumping and the complications of fracking. At the outset, these issues are not partisan; they bring to light corruption and disclose the ways white working-class people have been ignored and their concerns pushed aside (remember Gest's and Cramer's findings). Usually these actions prioritize the need for government reform. Levison contends that there is a "niche" in the heartland where citizens can organize on behalf of candidates and issues that represent alternatives to free market fundamentalism and various forms of exclusion and intolerance. In keeping with Levison's findings—with one exception—we look in on very

10. Levison, "Is There a Viable Progressive Strategy?"

11. Ibid.

important organizing going on in small-town and rural communities by the Missouri Rural Crisis Center (MRCC).

County Government and Local Control

At the beginning of this chapter we reported Benjamin Barber's conviction that organized social change needs to focus on the cities and city hall because of the dysfunction of state and federal government. In my conversations with Roger Allison and Tim Gibbons of the Missouri Rural Crisis Center (MRCC) I discovered a striking parallel with Barber's. In rural and small-town Missouri, a major issue is local control and the basic problem of big corporate America overrunning local communities and stripping them of democratic participation in fundamental issues affecting their lives. One basic part of this is Big Agriculture bringing in massive, absentee-controlled corporate factory farms that local people find detrimental to their quality of life, water and air, property rights and property values, and the sheer livability of their communities. These local people understand and have seen firsthand how corporate control has decimated rural counties in Missouri.

In 2016, MRCC beat back an attempt by a concentrated animal feeding operation (CAFO), the Pipestone System based in Pipestone, Minnesota. The plan of this feeding operation was to place 7,900 hogs and pigs on twenty acres with three buildings. The operation would require that manure be "stored in concrete pits below the buildings' floors that would [then] be applied on 1,300 acres. This size operation could produce approximately 4 million gallons of waste per year."[12]

In response, MRCC called for a new healthcare ordinance, pointing out that CAFOs had no obligation to local people, the county, or their communities. MRCC also let Howard County residents know that the state standards in Missouri legally allowed up to 17,499 hogs within two thousand feet of residents and that there were no limits on the number of hogs beyond three thousand feet. (You can imagine who lobbied through the state legislature these "standards.") Further, MRCC reported that there

---

12. "CAFO Threatens Howard County," Missouri Rural Crisis Center publication, 2016.

were "no setbacks from population areas" and that CAFOs with fewer than 17,500 hogs were not subject to the state's air quality standards. Furthermore, prevailing state standards allowed "waste from CAFOs to be applied 50 feet from [local residents'] property." For these reasons MRCC called upon the county commissioners to provide commonsense safeguards by means of a health ordinance "to protect our families, our communities, our health and our property rights and values."[13]

Building on more than twenty years of organizing in rural Missouri, MRCC passed around petitions (that supported a county health ordinance), got people to call the Howard County commissioners, attended public meetings, and held meetings with and put pressure on county commissioners in order to beat back the Pipestone proposal. In doing so, they were able to create and pass a community health ordinance and by that act halted the Pipestone plan. In Missouri these health ordinances are the only tools that local people and their representatives have to resist corporate farm invasions. For fifteen years MRCC has battled tooth and nail to maintain local control and "to have the ability to protect their citizens from the negative impact of corporate factory farms." Meanwhile, the Big Ag lobbyists have worked "vehemently" to cancel out local control of these corporate factory farms. That MRCC has been able to fight off these corporate maneuvers has been a major organizing victory.[14]

Still, MRCC is under no illusions about the near or distant future. This organizing and action effort must continue. The encroachments and the demands for privilege, benefits, and subsidies by corporate America are incessant. As we have seen, their talk of the free market is little more than a cover for their political and economic attempts at monopoly and control. The emphasis that MRCC places on the issue of working with people of color is important to note here. In a discussion of the declining life expectancy and health of people in rural Missouri and in communities of color, an MRCC memo laments the lack of "investments in voter programs" and the fact that so many progressive political organizations

---

13. Ibid.

14. Unpublished memo, Missouri Rural Crisis Center. Public document provided to me by Tim Gibbons, MRCC Communications Director.

have "de-prioritized" both rural Americans and communities of color (the latter, of course, exist in rural America).

A consequence of this is that these "non-prioritized" people go into "cycles of voter apathy and low turnout." The memo reports, for example, that forty-five thousand African-American Missourians who voted in 2012 did not do so in 2016, constituting 13 percent of the black electorate. The memo contends this shift was because their issues, like those of rural America, were not high on progressive agendas. In rural white communities MRCC found that former economic populists became conservative, a trend that has worsened as progressive platforms "have recently embraced a more pro-corporate agriculture agenda to the detriment of independent family farmers and families who live in rural Missouri."

The MRCC warning is right on target: if we ignore "the lived priorities and shared narratives of local residents" we should not be surprised by "politically opportunistic populist messaging tinged in racist rhetoric that has gained traction in Missouri, shifting electoral outcomes and voter preferences, and illuminating the need to organize white rural voters, working class voters, and voters of color simultaneously and at scale."[15] It would be difficult to state the issue more clearly.

I shared with Roger Allison and Tim Gibbons the research of people who find that white working-class people do not vote their interests but rather vote their culture and identity. Gibbons generally disagreed with this notion, contending that the dichotomy of culture and interest is not completely true. In the organizing experience of MRCC, he said that this is a false narrative. As we talked, what loomed very large with the MRCC was the issue of local control and the sense that farmers and other rural people are alarmed and incensed at the takeover of their communities by big corporate interests. Gibbons states that rural Missourians indeed *will* organize around their interests and have done so.

Furthermore, I shared with them Barber's conviction that we needed to focus on the cities and city hall in order to get real change and to counter the failures of representative government at both the state and federal

---

15. Unpublished memo from the Integrated Voter Engagement (IVE) effort of the Missouri Rural Crisis Center. Public document provided to me by Tim Gibbons, MRCC Communications Director.

level. Allison and Gibbons both pointed to a parallel in their organizing work regarding the necessity for efforts like theirs targeting county government and the county courthouse, suggesting that these were the crucial avenues for action in rural Missouri.[16]

These last comments of Allison and Gibbons represent a variation from some of the findings we found in other studies. Yet, there is continuity here. Where other studies have found people feeling powerless and shunted to the periphery of importance in the wider community, it makes sense that a threat to local control and the opportunity to make appeal to county commissioners, and therefore to a more accessible body, opens up an important consideration for community action and, yes, for an appeal to the interests of the community. It strikes me as well that this appeal of local control does not fly in the face of identity and culture but, indeed, coincides with them. In fact, it seems as though we have here a conjunction of identity, culture, tradition, locality, and local control. This may well be one of the most powerful forms of legitimacy available. Learning from this case study, therefore, may be of first-order importance.

With this in mind, we turn to an urban situation where some of these same factors were at work. What makes this case interesting is that it occurred in Colorado Springs, Colorado, a city known for its right-wing, reactionary citizenry and government.

Colorado Springs, Colorado

Recently Jim Hightower, that wonderful contemporary muckraker, reported on Colorado Springs and political change wrought by people there who were finally fed up with the dominating rule of right-wing forces. Colorado Springs is well-known as a bastion of right-wing, reactionary, extremist politics. It is the headquarters of some seventy Christian evangelical organizations from fundamentalist to the inerrancy-oriented sort. These extremist organizations are not the buckle of the Bible Belt but more like one of its political swords. In addition, Colorado Springs has,

---

16. Telephone conversation with MRCC Communications Director Tim Gibbons on November 30, 2017.

as Hightower reports, "a swarm of rabid anti-tax, anti-union, anti-gay, anti-Obama Republican front groups funded by corporate extremists." It is also home to the US Air Force Academy and four more military installations where some sixty-five thousand soldiers and civilians work. The city has one daily newspaper, *The Gazette*, owned by Philip Anschutz, whom Hightower characterizes as "a multibillionaire buddy of the Koch Brothers." The editorial pages of the paper are much like what I call "Fox Fictional News," promoting "alternative facts" and right-wing proposals. Furthermore, the city has, as Hightower describes it, "a paternalistic downtown establishment of politically connected developers who, incredibly, tout themselves as the 'moderates.'"[17]

But, says Hightower, its residents also include "a hardy band of progressives," including environmentalists, unionists, women's champions, scrappy entrepreneurs, LGBTQ activists, students and teachers, a sizeable immigrant population, social justice church groups, some sensible libertarians—and, importantly, a vibrant alternative newsweekly, *The Colorado Springs Independent*. This news weekly is engaged in investigative journalism and maintains its independence. Until recently, however, its victories have been few in the political climate of Colorado Springs.[18]

In 2016 the founder of *The Independent*, John Weiss, who had just retired from the paper as its publisher, was convinced that more could be done in the community. He began "a listening tour" with active community people and discovered a broad progressive consensus on any number of economic and environmental matters. Also, last year, Bernie Sanders easily came out victor in the county's Democratic caucus, and Sanders had caught the attention of both young voters and older working-class people. Weiss felt that the political atmosphere of Colorado Springs was changing and that the time might be right for new coalitions and for a progressive-populist movement.

Thus began the exploration of new strategies by a central group of community allies seeking to develop a new "political organizing effort" in

---

17. Jim Hightower, "You'll Be Gobsmacked by the Populist Victories Won in This Conservative Colorado Town," *The Hightower Lowdown*, July 19, 2017, https://hightowerlowdown.org/article/colorado-springs/.

18. Ibid.

the city. In a critical assessment of their previous efforts they identified two weaknesses. First was the tendency to operate primarily from a defensive posture, where they largely reacted to the ways the right wing framed issues, with the result that they spent too much time arguing against wrongful information and "dirty tricks." Second, developers and the right wing employed permanent staff and campaigned continually on their issues whereas progressives "started every battle from scratch" and then struggled to organize new action groups, which suffered from "a lack of institutional memory."[19]

This emerging group of political organizers' next step was to build a broad coalition of forces across the Pikes Peak region. This coalition included Democrats, unionists, supporters of Bernie Sanders, Greens, and even nonpartisan issue advocates. They sought out "fair-minded, commonsense moderates and sensible libertarians who were embarrassed both by religious crazies (whose intolerance sparked the town's moniker: 'Hate City') and by the political toadies of the area's corporate kingdom." The point was to build an ongoing organization committed to social change.

This coalition knew that "business-friendly cronies" had worked city government to advance the special interests of power elites while ignoring pressing community needs. In the spring and summer of 2016, they had more than one hundred local organizations and community activists committed to the achievement of one goal: "to mobilize a broad coalition around the progressive values and common interest proposals and then to assemble the full-time staff, tools, and resources needed to initiate and win candidate and issue campaigns."

In October seven local activists organized Together for Colorado Springs (T4CS). The coalition was made up of a diverse group: local entrepreneurs, digital specialists, unionists, and seasoned civil rights and environmental organizers. They organized working committees in order to turn their ideas into concrete, workable action. When Donald Trump won the presidency in November, more moderates and progressives joined T4CS in response.

---

19. Ibid., 2.

Public announcement of the coalition was made by means of "a wang-dang-doodle of a party," and Hightower observes that grassroots organizing of a democratic sort cannot just be sustained by relentless political action. It requires "social and cultural events" to complement its drawing power, bond its members, and manifest its democratic esprit. At the party a celebrative crowd of six hundred filled a local theater for an evening "of funky music, tub thumping speeches, and a renewal of hope—plus, of course, plentiful libations to lubricate the new movement."[20]

Then they got "lucky" (my characterization) with the Strawberry Fields caper. Philip Anschutz worked out a deal with the mayor and city council to *give* him Strawberry Fields, a 180-plus-acre public park. Anschutz, worth twelve billion dollars, wanted the park to develop "an exclusive horse stable and event center on it to serve the wealthy swells (including Charles and David Koch) who paid top dollar for getaways at the nearby Broadmoor hotel and resort," also owned by Anschutz. The deal involved no money from Anschutz, but rather the trade of 370 acres that the Broadmoor owned in another location, basically worthless land in comparison to the prime property owned by Colorado Springs citizens.

This outrageous proposition by the mayor and city council infuriated the public, and two-thirds of the townspeople opposed the deal. Yet, in spite of massive popular opposition, the city council, encouraged by the business establishment, voted six to three to close the deal in Anschutz's favor.

Then in the spring of 2017 six city council seats went up for election. The business establishment, the superrich, the right-wing Christian groups, and their allies went into the campaign running people who would serve their interests. They had boatloads of money and expectations of winning all six seats on the ballot. But the T4CS got behind five quite different candidates. In District 1 they supported an incumbent who had raised important questions with the business community. In District 2 they endorsed a Catholic chaplain, formerly a lawyer, who loved Pope Francis and wanted fairness for the poor of the city. In District 3 they

---

20. Ibid.

backed wholeheartedly a well-liked businessman who resides near Strawberry Fields. In yet another district they ran a transit activist, a woman, who was also a Bernie Sanders supporter. Further, they supported a moderate Republican incumbent who had opposed the Strawberry Fields deal. And, finally, in the district controlled by the Tea Party and people even further to the right, the T4CS did not file a candidate.

In the election the T4CS ticket was outspent ten to one, but they pulled off a spectacular victory. The three candidates that T4CS endorsed and the two they had recommended were elected by good margins. These five new candidates then joined a progressive holdover who was not up for election, thus giving this "pragmatic-Progressive coalition" a two-thirds majority on the city council. One of T4CS's council winners was selected council president and another the mayor *pro temp*.[21]

Hightower reports that this new majority of the city council went immediately to work in pursuit of policies and programs that opposed corporate giveaways, beginning with a lawsuit to challenge the Strawberry Fields decision by the previous council. Further, they are pursuing renewable energy sources, disclosure of campaign contributions, more open public space, expanding public access to high-speed Internet service, and the welcoming of the LGBTQ community into city government.[22]

It strikes me that a number of factors are very important in examining the strategy utilized by the Colorado Springs coalition that led to the organizing effort of the T4CS: the listening tour; shifting political atmosphere; self-critique of past weaknesses of the coalition; building a well-staffed social change organization; bringing together a diverse political group of people; reaching out to and mobilizing some one hundred organizations including unions; the outrageous Strawberry Field caper; encouraging a diverse, new set of candidates to run for city council; and don't forget the party! Not bad for a flyover city.

---

21. Ibid., 3.
22. Ibid., 4.

Referendums versus Representative Government

Minimum Wage

Several years ago, before I had read Benjamin Barber's proposals for focusing political action on the cities, the Reverend Sam Mann expressed his judgment that we could no longer count on representative government to get the changes we desperately need in Kansas City. Mann, a white Alabamian who served as pastor to a black church in the inner city for more than forty years, has a reputation among many African Americans in the city of being actually "a black man." Because of his frustration with government, and because of the very low minimum wage in Missouri, he and four other Kansas Citians—I was one of those—put together an initiative petition calling for increases in the minimum wage within the city. The petition required raising the minimum wage from $7.25 to $10 an hour upon passage. It then called for increases over the next four years to a minimum of $15 an hour with that amount subsequently pegged to cost of living increases.

Our proposal triggered opposition from some business groups with the result that the city council passed a resolution based on lower increases in the minimum rates. But our community action groups, not being satisfied with these lesser rates, still filed for a citywide referendum on the minimum wage and took it to the voters. We won with nearly 70 percent of the vote. But not long after this victory the state legislature passed a bill that denied any city or other political entity the right to raise its minimum wage above that of the state of Missouri, thus nullifying the new city council resolution and the 70 percent city referendum by the citizens of Kansas City, Missouri.

In response, a coalition of community groups started collecting signatures for a statewide referendum on the minimum wage in 2018. We are also working with legal sources to determine whether we have any recourse through the courts to the action of the state legislature, with attention to possible implications for this issue based on the Ninth and Tenth Amendments of the US Constitution. Meanwhile, the city council is working on a resolution that would require all businesses doing work with the city itself to pay a minimum wage of $10 an hour. The city council is pushing for businesses in the city to voluntarily pay a minimum wage of $10 an hour, thus circumventing the state legislature's action banning an official minimum wage. In addition, community groups are gathering signatures for a statewide referendum. Because of general support for raising the minimum wage across the country, the group has hope for a positive outcome in this effort. This work illustrates quite clearly the kind of local community action aimed at city hall, as Barber suggests, but also the importance of referenda for community action.

The "Clean Missouri" Initiative

We turn next to yet one other illustration that relates directly not only to the white working class but points in an important direction for the future. As indicated above, the great majority of the Missouri legislature is bought off by billionaires, corporate money, and right-wing lobbyists. As reported, there are no limits on campaign finance in Missouri, and all you have to do is to follow the money to know how the great majority of our legislators will vote.

Presently, coalitions of social action groups are working across the state to get signatures on two referenda. One of those is called the Clean Missouri Initiative. With sufficient registered voter signatures, we can place this initiative on the ballot in 2018. The referendum would put the following requirements before the voters, making for significant legislative reform.

The referendum ensures that legislative records will be open and that elected officials must wait two years after their legislative terms before taking lobbyist jobs. It eliminates 99 percent or more of lobbying gifts by limiting them to $5. By having nonpartisan experts redraw legislative districts to be reviewed by a citizen commission, it will end gerrymandering. Amid a number of other needed requirements, it will also reduce campaign contribution to General Assembly candidates to $2,500 for the senate and $2,000 for the house.[23]

23. The Clean Missouri Initiative. Accessed October 4, 2017, http://www.cleanmissouri.org/solution/.

Gathering signatures for a referendum such as this one is always difficult, but desperately important to correct big money influenced government. Further, the kind of coalition building going on across the state will pay real dividends on future actions. Not only are large numbers of people and organizations getting to know each other, they are learning how to work together. There is also an active organization called The Faith Labor Alliance that is connecting clergy and labor leaders in common causes. This opens up opportunity for people of color and white working people to act together politically; and, just as important in a state like Missouri, it enables urban and rural people to work on common concerns, which in light of Cramer's research could pay both relational and power dividends. Such organizing work certainly can fulfill an old adage that an organized people can beat organized money on issues of this kind.

"Right to Work" Laws

We are also getting signatures from registered voters for a second referendum to abolish the "right to work" law passed by our state legislators. Once again, the legislature's action was designed to further weaken labor unions in our state and place working people all the more at the mercy of the superrich, corporate America, and right-wing partisans.

The important thing here is to see the kind of coalition work that is going on between labor unions, civil rights groups, citizen action groups, and others. Important to this work has also been the coming together of faith and labor groups. Directions like these are crucial to overcome the inequities of class and race and to build a justice of the common good.

The Reverend William Barber and Fusion Politics

Yet another form of grassroots, bottom-up action has been going on in the state of North Carolina. Under the leadership of the Reverend William J. Barber II, the Moral Mondays movement has had extraordinary success in organizing, protesting through civil obedience, and effecting social change. Putting together highly intentional interfaith and secular groups, Rev. Barber describes their work as "fusion politics," illustrating "the power of coalition."[24] He describes this effort as neither Republican nor Democrat, neither liberal nor conservative, but rather one that pursues a moral agenda "for all that is good and right."[25] Refusing an "acceptable" injustice, the movement stands up against the forces of domination and captivity at work in North Carolina.[26]

This effort began with a process of listening, of hearing each other into voice—giving people the opportunity to speak and to be heard. People told their stories to one another and began to build relationships. Through this process they identified "fourteen justice tribes" in North Carolina that included groups as diverse as those working for a living wage, public financing of elections, environmental issues, civil rights enforcement, and opposition to the so-called *war on terror*.

These groups called for "a People's Assembly" at the state house, a major teach-in that included a march of citizens in February 2007. Marshaling together a fourteen-point agenda, they posted them on a fourteen-foot-high placard just outside the state legislative building.[27] They took the name "Historic Thousands on Jones Street" (HKonJ) because a coalition of such diversity had never before taken their concerns to the state house.[28]

Part of HKonJ's advocacy work was to get out the vote, and in 2008 all fifteen of North Carolina's electoral college votes went to Barack Obama. This had not happened since Ronald Reagan's presidential victory in 1980. In 2007, some 185,000 new voters were registered, and Obama won that election by a little more than 100,000 votes.[29]

---

24. The Rev. Dr. William J. Barber II with Jonathan Wilson Hartgrove, *The Third Reconstruction: Moral Mondays, Fusion Politics, and the Rise of a New Justice Movement* (Boston: Beacon Press, 2016), 41.

25. Ibid., 52.

26. Ibid., 45–46.

27. Ibid., 51.

28. The state legislative building in Raleigh, North Carolina, is located on Jones Street.

29. Barber and Hartgrove, *The Third Reconstruction*, 54.

This opened up HKonJ to a powerful attack by right-wing extremists who had a great deal of money and power on their side, including an ultraconservative multimillionaire businessman, who committed to "a takeover of North Carolina's government." He provided roughly three million of the thirty million dollars in campaign finance for reactionary Republicans running for the state house of representatives. Through the use of "the politics of fear" they won a majority of the seats.[30]

After the election, North Carolina's new Republican State Speaker of the House, Thom Tillis, was captured on video revealing his attitudes to a group of white people: "We have to find a way to divide and conquer the people who are on assistance." He went on to say that he wanted "a woman with cerebral palsy who 'deserves' government assistance to look down on those people who, unlike her, choose to be in the condition they're in and therefore deserve nothing." Barber saw this resistance of the powers that be as confirmation of the moral cause of the HKonJ coalition's fusion politics. He knew the extremists would fight back with all the clout they had "because we were strong."[31]

Meanwhile, through the movement's fusion politics, former enemies in North Carolina became "co-laborers for the common good."[32] They realized that their work "was primarily cultural [note!], not political." Their opposition had come up with vocabulary like "entitlements," "big government," and "the undeserving poor." To counter these, the coalition needed "powerful images of solidarity." They needed "daily acts of justice and community building."[33]

The coalition then had success organizing workers at a hog processing plant. Labor organizing had been going on there for a decade, but the five thousand workers, mostly people of color, had been "intimidated, attacked, and harassed by the factory boss." In the media and the larger

---

30.   Ibid., 63.

31.   Ibid., 64. For the video of Tillis's remarks, see "NC House Speaker Tillis: Divide and Conquer!" on YouTube. https://www.youtube.com/watch?v=O8ewESI51s4.

32.   Barber and Hartgrove, *The Third Reconstruction*, 67.

33.   Ibid., 68.

community, however, the issue was seen as simply a matter of opposition between business and labor.

But the coalition changed that narrative by enabling workers to tell their own stories. As the plant tried to drive a wedge between the black and brown workers, the HKonJ coalition joined the workers to resist this tactic and to stand with strength together. These efforts provided an alternative narrative so that "the public story was no longer one about workers versus bosses, but rather about the moral challenge of people receiving the just fruit of their labor, a principle enshrined in our state Constitution." With this, Barber notes, the union finally signed a good contract with management, and "the relationship between our coalition and labor unions was deepened."[34]

Not everything the coalition did succeeded; the far right, now holding power in the state legislature and the governor's office, began passing legislation to suppress voting, allow fracking, cut the budget for social programs, promote regressive tax measures and increase taxes for other citizens, reverse a law allowing death row black inmates to challenge their convictions on the basis of racial discrimination, make cuts to public education, and other extremist measures. Barber acknowledges that 2013 was a very difficult time.

But then began the Moral Monday witness. A group of the HKonJ folks went to the state legislature "to instruct our legislators about the evil they were committing despite the fact that they refused to meet with us."[35] This resulted in the arrest of seventeen members of the coalition and triggered a rallying cry across the fourteen issue groups and their membership so that twice as many people were arrested the next week, which fueled the protest. For thirteen Mondays, thousands of people demonstrated against the legislature's extremist measures. Barber reports that "a new kind of revival had taken hold of us," not unlike the camp meetings of the Third Great Awakening in the late nineteenth century of American history.[36]

34. Ibid., 70.

35. Ibid., 101.

36. Ibid, 103.

The protests took on a liturgical character with the singing of songs, testimony, and opportunities for the poor and vulnerable to be heard from the platform. People who were both Republican and Democrat reported on how the legislature had cut off their unemployment benefits. Further, as Barber relates, these Moral Mondays featured "economists, public policy experts, and lawyers to lay out our agenda and explain how it would work."[37]

Reverend Barber continually emphasizes that this is a moral movement, an effort that supports the common good of all, not just the rich and the powerful. Their platform has been primarily one to support the poor and those who are hurting so that the vulnerable can be heard. Their work is not finished, and they continue to fight resistance from the powers; but they sustain a significant struggle now cropping up in other states, opening new initiatives for a morally-centered effort and strategic direction. Presently, a new Poor People's movement is organized for 2018 and beyond.

In Sum and Conclusion

We moved in this chapter to work on community action, especially on coalition efforts that involved white working people in urban and rural locations. These efforts can address the isolation and marginality that many white working people experience, and offer opportunities to work with people of color. In addition, actions aimed at city hall, the county courthouse, and the state legislature provide tangible, meaningful options for building the common good. Along with these, single-issue campaigns and local and state referenda can be significant arenas for grassroots action. Further, crucial change directions are available for the heartland, including hard-right cities and states, especially around extremist right-wing misdeeds and economic issues. Finally, the uses of cultural traditionalism and family rhetoric are crucial to advance and legitimate community organizing, along with the central role of moral concerns in grassroots action.

37. Ibid., 105.

There is yet one more thing to do, and that is to move to theological reflections on what has gone before. How does one do theology with white working-class people? Is there any relationship between that barrel of working-class cultural resources and theological thought and spiritual direction? I believe there is, so we head there in the next chapter.

CHAPTER 8

BIBLICAL AND THEOLOGICAL REFLECTIONS

In this final chapter I return to the cultural traditionalism of white working-class America, a characteristic we have identified in a number of places above. Here we will focus biblically and theologically on morality and family rhetoric, patriotism and love of country, the Bible and the nations, the military and working-class support for our troops, and free enterprise and the American system of government. Each of these represents a significant challenge to the Christian tradition and requires some clarity about how these matters can be addressed theologically.

A biblical and theological approach takes on importance, in part, because the great majority of white working-class people in America are Christian, at least nominally. The largest plurality of them is evangelical with significant participation in mainline and Catholic churches. I personally come at these issues as a Christian and a mainline church person.

Further, in community organizing I have found it important for people to speak out of their particular faith traditions for two reasons. First, our faith traditions are the places from which our deepest convictions come. Moving up the ladder of abstraction to find some "spiritual principles" of such generality as to cover everyone actually speaks for *no one*. Second, as a Christian, it strikes me as the height of arrogance even to suggest that

God has chosen to reveal God's Self in our tradition alone. Yes, I believe that God is revealed definitively in Israel and in Jesus Christ—that's why I am a Christian. But to suggest that our tradition is the exclusive revelatory work and action of God is a claim we are not able to make. Christians are on far better ground to reach out in love and respect of those who are *other* and to seek to discover what God is doing there.

Church and Culture

Not surprisingly, the relationship of the Christian faith to a given culture or subculture has been an issue from the very beginning of the church; indeed, from the start of the ministry and mission of Jesus. Even as a Jew himself, Jesus entered early on into conflict with the religious authorities of his own tradition. That he was crucified on a Roman cross suggests clearly that he had gotten crosswise with the imperial government that oppressed his own country.

At the same time, Jesus embodied and expressed a great range of the discourses and practices of his day. He was a Jew; and his teachings, as we have them in the New Testament, come directly from the Hebrew text, selective though they may be or perhaps reflecting a tradition or traditions within the interpretations of the First Testament in his time. He spoke and taught in an idiom, Aramaic. His teachings used images and illustrations from the world about him: fishermen, sowers, workers of the field, Samaritans, rich men, a woman who searches for a pearl of great price, a poor widow who gives out of the very substance of her life, and others. He was a Galilean, the son of Mary with a father who was a carpenter, and he came from the "flyover town" of Nazareth. Yet the Gospel of John says that he was the Word made flesh and dwelt (pitched his tent) with us.

Even in the birth of the church, that great conglomeration of people was "speaking in their native languages," and yet those gathered heard them "declaring the mighty works of God in our own languages!" (Acts 2:6, 11). With regard to the proclamation of the gospel, the apostle Paul made use of the literary conventions of his own time. The diatribe, letter forms of communication, and Paul's knowledge of modes of argumentation in the Greco-Roman world are clearly reflected in his writing.

Across the history of the church the ongoing struggle to proclaim an authentic gospel and to connect it to the various peoples around the world has been incessant.[1] It is important in this regard to be reminded that the church that reaches out to other cultures is always already in yet some other culture itself. More specifically, for our purposes, we must continually be on guard against believing that some highly literate, even academic, professional and business middle-class church possesses the authentic gospel and reaches out to working-class people more accommodated to "the world" and somehow less in their appropriation and expression of the gospel.

The question for any church in its engagement with the discourses and other material practices of any culture concerns how these activities are transformed by the gospel. One theologian suggests that we must both "borrow from a given cultural idiom and bend and shape that idiom in such a way that it becomes a fit instrument for the communication of the gospel."[2] He states:

> The evangelical strategy does not accept being walled into a ghetto by the outside world. Not only does it accept the language of the environs: it seizes it, expropriates it, and uses it to say things that could not have been said in its prior language; nor could they have been said by anyone else using the world's wider language."[3]

---

1. I appreciate very much the social and cultural history of Christianity by Howard Clark Kee, et al., because of the close attention they give to the continual interaction of the church with the various cultures it encounters across its history. See *Christianity: A Social and Cultural History* (New York: Macmillan, 1991).

2. See Douglas Harink, *Paul among the Postliberals: Pauline Theology beyond Christendom and Modernity* (Grand Rapids, MI: Brazos Press, 2003), 138–41, especially 139. I am indebted here to Douglas Harink for his concise summary of John Howard Yoder's position on borrowing and bending. Further, I deeply grieve recent revelations of Yoder's sexual abuse of women in the course of his career. I grieve for Yoder, that his theological and ethical contributions will now forever be called into question by this failure of character; but I grieve especially for the women, many of whom were under his professorial tutelage and certainly disempowered by his extraordinary charisma and presence. On Yoder's sexual abuse, see Rich Preheim, "Report Reveals Full History of Theologian's Abuse, Institutions' Response," *The Christian Century*, February 17, 2015.

3. John Howard Yoder, "On Not Being Ashamed of the Gospel," 296. Quoted in Harink, *Paul among the Postliberals*, 139.

So, as we examine the cultural traditionalism of white working-class Americans, we ask these questions: In what ways can these cultural patterns be affirmed? How and where should they be opposed? How may they be borrowed and bent in a transforming direction? How may we seize the categories of these cultural commitments and hammer them into shapes faithful to Christ?[4]

To begin, I want to place white working traditional conservatism in a more comprehensive vision of life and hope. This is not an attempt to take away the idiom of the white working-class world but to fulfill that idiom in ultimate claims.

Morality, Relational Thinking, and Family Rhetoric

Morality plays a central role in the lives of white working-class people in several of our studies; and clearly, there is much to affirm about morality with this important group of people. It plays a crucial role in the structuring of social order, but it also has serious problems as a way of making distinctions between and determining "us and them." My first move is to address this practice of morality within the family rhetoric of working-class life. That is, we can use the relational thinking of working-class people both to affirm the value of and raise question with the family. Sometimes the focus on family is simply too narrow; it deals too exclusively with "me and mine." The way to challenge this narrowness is to use family rhetoric to open up and extend the relationships under consideration.

I think of the importance of speaking about Jesus not only as our Lord and Savior but as our brother as well. That he was so fully human is clear; and he himself declared that his mother, brothers, and sisters were those who shared in his work (Matt 12:46-50). I think about the fact that he was one of us; he shared our plight. He was probably for a time—like his father—a carpenter; and in all likelihood knew what hard work was.

---

4. John Howard Yoder, *The Priestly Kingdom: Social Ethics as Gospel* (Notre Dame, IN: University of Notre Dame Press, 1984), 54.

Without question he knew suffering and death. Yes, he is Lord of lords and King of kings, and he is above all nations. This is the antidote to idolatrous patriotism and the poisons that would make the nation-state the meaning of history.

Family rhetoric not only works with one's own family but can also extend and work with the families of others. I have already mentioned the importance of the local congregation as an extended family. But a family rhetoric can reach out even further, for example, in working with that great text from Acts, "From one person God created every human nation to live on the whole earth" (17:26), which speaks to us of the ground level, created kinship of all people.

So, with respect to those who are other, family rhetoric can expand family ties to the full compass of those who suffer and are in need; in other words, seeing the face of Christ, our Lord and our brother, in people who are other so that by this reality they become brother and sister. By kinship in Christ I mean a relationship that refuses the walls of exclusion. It is an alternative family to the hostilities of the world.

We have reported research that language such as "multiculturalism" and "diversity" do not work very well with most working-class people. They sense in such language a kind of relativism, and they often are not incorrect. More than that, words such as *multicultural* and *diversity* are the language of the college-trained and represent the kind of talk working-class people associate with the fancy language of people who think they are "sophisticated."

When, however, the conversation turns to the families of people who are other—real mothers and fathers, real sons and daughters—and the struggles they have that are similar, at least in some ways, to their own, then the logics of their thought can shift. I do not mean to suggest that this is a fail-safe practice, but it is a far more effective one than the rationales that come out of high-literacy or management-speak or the professional savoir faire of the upper middle class.

For example, I am active with Stand Up KC and Jobs with Justice in Kansas City, pushing for a minimum wage of $15 an hour and a union. This movement has increased the wages of two million low wage workers in the United States. An interracial effort, it has focused primarily but not only on fast-food workers. At rallies and demonstrations workers tell their personal stories, stories of people who work two or three jobs because they cannot get a full-time job in these industries. Employers do not want to pay the benefits required for full-time employees, and they want workers only for busy times. This necessitates fast-food workers taking on two and sometimes three part-time jobs and trying to manage work schedules, childcare, family time, and just rest and sleep.

I find not only how similar the stories are but the kind of impact they have across race. Black, white, and brown working people struggle with so many similar challenges, and they organize together because they are so much in the same boat. Not only is it difficult to argue with each of their stories, but they are so telling in the way they decimate popular misinformation and false images of the working poor. Their testimonies about their families and the ongoing, unending, grinding hassle to provide for their children and pay their bills energize action and enable coalitions across class, race, and gender.

Theologically speaking, it is a very short step from talking about the families of others to their being encompassed in the family of God. It is hard to cut out other people as "them" when they are placed in family rhetoric in the household of God. I have seen with my own eyes many times what happens when talk about "poverty cheats" and "welfare queens" is countered by a story about Wilbur's sister or cousin Margie, who "have had a hard time." Moreover, this family rhetoric can cut across the lines of race, not by some alchemy of high literacy, but by a family idiom caught up in the grace and love of God.

Family rhetoric can even reach out to nature. Saint Francis was ahead of us all as he named and praised sun, moon, and stars, and winged creatures and four-legged ones, as brothers and sisters. His family rhetoric could encompass the entire creation. I find a great love of forests and waterways, birds and animals, land and sea among working people. This can take on a richer meaning with the words and thoughts of someone like Saint Francis.

But talk alone—even family rhetoric—is not enough; and extended family, taken alone, won't do it. Sensibility requires community. This is where the language of the church as *family* takes on major importance. To model the church as extended family, to relate to each other as brothers and sisters in Christ, is to offer a range of practices for the building of a faithful congregation. To be sure, these practices cannot merely be borrowed and instituted; they must be "bent," sometimes "hammered" into shape, but the rich density of such indigenous practices brings abundant offerings for curvature into the liturgies of worship and the Eucharist and the doxologies in service and justice to the wider community.

Still, there is more here to be spelled out. When a church uses familiar language or engages in practices that people know "in their bones," there is a sense of being home, of welcome, of belonging, and of affirmation. When these are lifted up in the presence of God's blessing and beauty, there is an offering of morality and value of such scale and depth that no other gift can provide.

To people who have been as ignored, dismissed, and stigmatized as white working-class Americans, the experience of being swept up in the acceptance of God in a family-like church can provide a redemptive identity and the strength to face the uncertainties and struggles of dealing with a postindustrial world.

While the great majority of white working-class people in United States are Christian, at least nominally, millions of them are alienated from the church—in no small part because they feel as if they are strangers without a home and people without an invitation. A baptized family rhetoric and indigenous practices arced into the biblical story and faithfulness to God may well be the single most evangelistic move the church can make.

Patriotism and Love of Country

Patriotism is an important part of traditional conservatism in the barrel of cultural resources of most working-class white Americans. Without question, love of country can be both a good thing and a problem. Love of country can take on the status of an idol. It can be an inordinate love that leads to excesses and extremes, to militarism, to an ethos of violence, and to a regimented mindset. At the same time, love of country can also be important and valuable. To love this land, to love its people, does not require that it be idolized. Love of country does not have to be nativist. It does not have to be xenophobic or white supremacist. It depends on who is family and how wide is the reach of those to whom we belong.

During my lifetime I have spoken in all fifty states in the US. I can close my eyes and see stretches of land in every one of them: the shoreline of Rhode Island; the woods of rural Wisconsin; the lakes of Minnesota; and the piney woods of Mississippi. I can see sunflower fields in Kansas and stretches of bluebonnets in central Texas; the Rockies and the plains of Colorado; the long ridges of Wyoming; the hollers and hills of Appalachia; the spectacular beauty of Alaska; and the surf and shore of Hawaii. I can see the cities of New York, Chicago, Los Angeles, Atlanta, San Francisco, Dallas, Phoenix, and the rolling hills of Kansas City; there are grasslands of cattle, horses, buffalo, sheep, and elk.

One of my favorite forms of meditation is to let my mind range over these memories. To do so is to love and appreciate the variations of contour and climate, of color and vegetation, of life in its many forms, and of its mix of people: Anglo and African American, Latino and Native American, white Ethnic Europeans and gold-skinned Asian Americans; and the growing mixtures of all of these and more. What a country!

In so many ways it is easy to love this country. When in these meditations I think of the goodness of creation and this country as an expression of that goodness and all that God has done. I think of the need to love and protect this land from despoliation and pollution, from the rape of the mountains and the poisoning of the rivers and underground water. I think of blue skies and clean rain, and air one can breathe. To love the land, its animals and people, its fish and fowl, and to do so with ecological integrity, is to embody the teaching of a good creation; it is to proclaim and practice the goodness of what God has made.

And yet, and yet... there is so much we dare not forget: the genocide of Native Americans; the slavery and manifestations of white supremacy against African Americans; the long and unremitting exploitation of the white working class; the colonialism and systemic aggression against Latinos; the overt and covert suppression of and violence against women and the denial of their very citizenship until the twentieth century; the persecutory stigmatization of LGBTQ people; and the ghettoization and stifling of immigrant populations. There is more, but the naming of these violations indicates something of how much there is to be done.

So how do we address love of country and love of place theologically? I suggest immediately above that we place love of country in a strong doctrine of creation in which we express gratitude for its goodness as a gift from God. At the same time, we must not forget the profound damage done in our national life by making idols of our nation-state. To deal with the dangers of the idolatry of the state, we turn to biblical teaching regarding the nations. These should provide us with an appropriate sense of political authority, on one hand, and an extravagant antidote to the idolatry of the nation, on the other.

The Bible and the Nations

Our comments here will be far too brief, but the biblical text offers powerful perspectives on government very much needed by all of us in our own time, and no less so by the white working class. Let's begin with the New Testament and then work back to the Hebrew text. There are two passages that capture the sweep of the New Testament views of government, Romans 13 and Revelation 13.

In Romans 13 Paul says, "Every person should place themselves under the authority of the government. There isn't any authority unless it comes from God, and the authorities that are there have been put in place by God. So, anyone who opposes the authority is standing against what God has established" (verses 1-2a). Paul goes on to communicate that anyone who stands against government will be punished. The government does what it does for our benefit; it is God's servant. So, "it is necessary to place yourself under the government's authority, not only to avoid God's punishment but also for the sake of your conscience" (verses 2b-6).

In this brief space, just two comments about this passage can be made. The first is that these verses must be considered in the larger context within the book of Romans itself. For example, in Romans 12:2 Paul says, "Don't be conformed to the patterns of this world but be transformed by the renewing of your minds so that you can figure out what God's will is—what is good and pleasing and mature." Second, while Paul says that the people of the church in Rome should place themselves under the authority of the government, this does not literally call for obedience as such. To use the language of other translations of key words in this passage, *subordination* to the state does not mean necessarily *obedience*. For example, one can disobey the state, refusing obedience, but not attempt to avoid penalties resulting therefrom. This would be a case of being under the authority of but not obedient to the state.[5]

Revelation 13 is a radically different text. Here we find the famous mystical imagery of the beast rising up out of the sea, a passage that has been used to identify a host of actors as that beast. In my own lifetime I have heard it identified with Germany, Japan, Italy—in World War II— and with Russia, China, and the Middle East for half a century and more.

Sound biblical scholarship would agree with Brian K. Blount's reading in his account that "the beast is Rome." Moreover, according to Blount's reading of Revelation, "this bestial, imperial power is satanic." Blount also points out that the ten horns and seven heads of the beast are directly connected to Rome (17:3, 7, 9, 12, 16), and that the seven heads represent the seven hills and seven emperors of Rome. In the case of the seven emperors, the number seven indicates not merely one emperor, but because of the numeral's connotation of completeness conveys "the entire sense of Roman rule." And so, "the beast is the entire empire, and its economic, political, social dimension, and especially its religious, theological, and spiritual dimension."[6] My point here in contrasting Romans 13 and Rev-

---

5. See John Howard Yoder, *The Politics of Jesus* (Grand Rapids, MI: William B. Eerdmans, 1972), 193–214.

6. Brian K. Blount, *Revelation: A Commentary*, The New Testament Library (Louisville, KY: Westminster John Knox Press, 2009), 246. In this last sentence Blount is quoting Pablo Richard, *Apocalypse: A People's Commentary on the Book of Revelation* (Maryknoll, NY: Orbis Books, 1995), 114.

elation 13 is not to lift up some contradiction in scripture so that we may disbelieve it all on this particular topic of political rule. Rather, I report this to suggest very appropriate tensions within scripture itself that indicate the necessity for more than one response to ruling authorities.

Further, New Testament scholarship often observes that Paul's writing is occasional and addressed to specific situations and circumstances. To turn a comment of his on governing authorities into an absolute, fails to take into account that he is writing letters to congregations and addressing the challenges that a particular church faces at a particular time. Let me say even further that virtually all writing is occasional. To think otherwise is to visualize some author perched up on an Archimedean point of neutrality from which he or she can survey a total scene with utter transcendence. There is a wonderful working-class expletive for such arrogant pretense.

But let's move to a third New Testament passage in the book of Acts, where the apostles are performing "many signs and wonders among the people" (5:12a), especially healings. People bring "the sick out into the main streets and lay them on cots and mats so that at least Peter's shadow could fall on some of them as he passed by" (verse 15). The text says that the religious leadership of Jerusalem "was overcome with jealousy" (verse 17). So, the religious leaders have Peter and the disciples thrown into prison, but God has an angel of the Lord help them break jail! The angel then instructs Peter and the disciples to go back to the temple and to "tell the people everything about this new life" (verse 20). Note that they did not attempt to escape the scene or run from the authorities.

When the religious leadership is told that the disciples are out of jail, Peter and the others are brought back before them. These religious leaders call them into account, ordering the disciples not to teach in the name of Jesus, and exclaiming, "Look at you! You have filled Jerusalem with your teaching." Peter's answer is one that rings down through the centuries: "We must obey God rather than humans!" (verses 28-29). The ultimate authority of God takes precedence over all other claims.

Now let's turn to just two texts from the Old Testament, where we are "burdened" by a treasure house of stories and teachings about government. The extraordinary story of Exodus tells us that God hears the

145

cries and sees the suffering of the people of Israel and calls Moses to lead a brickyard revolt to set his people free. That God is a God of deliverance and liberation speaks powerfully from this text. My suggestion here is not that we are to engage in some slaphappy disregard of government and law. Here we need Paul's wisdom from the Romans 13. At the same time, there come those times when God's liberative action calls us to stand against the powers that be.

And, of course there is the ever-vital story in Daniel 3 with Shadrach, Meshach, and Abednego, who refuse to bow down to the statue of King Nebuchadnezzar of Babylon. For their refusal to do so, the king orders them thrown into a fiery furnace, but they are miraculously unharmed. A shocked Nebuchadnezzar orders the three to come out of the furnace. When they emerge unscathed, Nebuchadnezzar declares that "the God of Shadrach, Meshach, and Abednego be praised!" (verse 28). Once again, the biblical text exonerates those who obey God and stand up even to kings, especially those who would require idolatry from the people of God.

Finally, we go to Matthew 25: 31-46, where all the nations of the world will be gathered before "the Human One" ("the Son of Man," NRSV) in final judgment. They will be divided into sheep on his right side and goats on his left. The sheep who inherit the kingdom will be those who gave food to the hungry, drink to the thirsty, welcome to the stranger, clothes to the naked, who cared for the sick and visited those in prison because in these very acts they serve the King/the Human One himself. In contrast, the goats who failed to make these offerings to those in need turned away the Lord himself. "And they will go away into eternal punishment. But the righteous ones will go into eternal life" (verse 46).

The misuse of this text happens often because it is so typically read in individualistic terms. People fail to see that it is addressed to the *nations*, not to individuals. It is the nations who will be called to account, who will be judged by their failure to address human need, who will go into eternal punishment for their lack of compassion. There is no greater clarion call to the nations than the thunderous instruction and ultimate destiny pro-claimed in this text.

We could go on because there are other extraordinary claims about the nations of the world. For example, Isaiah tells us that "the nations are like a drop in a bucket, / and valued as dust on a scale" and that "all the nations are like nothing before God. / They are viewed as less than nothing and emptiness" (40:15a, 17). Yet in Revelation 21:24, in those last days when there will be a new heaven and a new earth, the nations will be in that final parade: "The nations will walk by its [God's] light, and the kings of the earth will bring their glory into it."

The biblical narrative provides rich teaching regarding the nations of the earth. Before God they are as nothing, as dust. They are not to be idolized but rather resisted in their pretenses of deification. Sometimes they require revolt and revolution. At other times, they require disobedience and jail because we are called finally to obey God and not human authority. Furthermore, the nations of the world will be judged ultimately by how they meet raw human need, even as they march in that final eschatological parade. And yet in the midst of all these teachings we are called to be subordinate to the ruling authorities, albeit in a biblical context of powerful and trenchant qualification.

So, what does this have to do with the white working class? The great majority of these people love their country and believe strongly in being patriotic. It is, if you will, one of the most powerful commitments and narratives of cultural traditionalism in the barrel of cultural resources. Love of country comes up in conversations, in practices such as the Pledge of Allegiance and the singing of the national anthem. It is often a first recourse when considering some national question. And, yes, it can be combined with Christian faith and discipleship in ways that take on divine status and therefore idolatrous character. So how do we address these in light of biblical teaching?

To begin, let it be said that love of one's nation, as such, is not denounced in scripture. An appropriate love of country is not questioned in the Bible; rather it is the attempt to give the nation ultimate status and to make it an idol that is condemned. It is the overreach of a governmental authority that is to be resisted even to the point of revolt. It is the insensitivity of the nations to human hurt and isolation that is to be challenged. So how do we work with these?

The first thing to be done is to bring greater awareness to working people of the full sweep of biblical teaching so that the nation-state is placed in that far more compelling and realistic scriptural account of the governments and rulers of the world.

Second, working people, like others in this country, need a far better understanding of our nation's history, both its achievements and its failures; the best of its ideals and its often wicked and unjust misuse of the land; of its nonhuman critters, its people, and even its children. I would begin this work with stories about white working people and the labor history of this country. In preaching and teaching I would lay this out not in a history book style, but in story format, so that they would be remembered, and so that the graphic violence, exploitation, abuse, and oppression of white working people would be clear. This means, for example, giving attention to white indentured servitude early on in the colonies.

I would tell stories of the labor movement itself and the violence against working people, of the use of "goon squads" by industrial owners; and I would tell stories of today's working people devastated by industrial closings and the people who suffer in their very concrete, ordinary lives from the injustices of the contextual factors outlined in this book in chapter 1.

There are also significant stories of farmers and farmworkers and their efforts to throw off the domination of powerful agricultural businesses and their power elite allies. Stories should at least initially take the side of working-class and rural people and thereby provide new clarity about the oppression and exploitation that have been pervasively present throughout our history. Stories such as these sharply call into question the idolatries of America and its immoral complicity in the violations against working people.

Third, I would also tell stories of times when black and white and brown workers formed coalitions and opened the possibilities of real change, only to be confronted with divide and conquer strategies by owners and other power elites to break up such coalitions. The elites knew that by working together the working-class could transform the unjust privilege, the meager wages, and the oppressive circumstances of their lives.[7]

The point here is that countering the idolatries of our nation with white working-class people is to be done not so much with statistics and analysis but with story and description. These are the structural core of their idiom and the passageway into their barrel of cultural resources.

Further, the case can be made that the purpose of the nation is not its own privilege; it is to serve the people. The people do not exist for the sake of the nation; the nation exists for the sake of the people. In addition, there is no messianic nation; we are not saved by the nation-state. When I die I am very clear that the American eagle will not swoop down and take me into eternal life in God.

Someone may say that the Bible is not important for all white working-class people, and I am aware of that, of course. But our focus in this section is on those for whom it *is* important, and perhaps a further word is necessary about the nature of that importance. The great majority of white working-class people are neither fundamentalist nor biblical "inerrantists." Rather, they have a basic *loyalty* to the Bible. They are irritated by those whose interpretations seem like attempts to get out from under its teaching.[8] During my work in ministry I have served a total of ten different congregations where a majority or near majority was composed of working-class urban and/or rural people. Without exception a great number of people within that majority had a firm sense of biblical authority but were not fundamentalists; yet they appreciated and took seriously the biblical witness.

---

7. Howard Zinn's *A People's History of the United States* (New York: Harper and Row, 1980) is a significant resource of labor and farm stories. It is a treasure house of illustrations for the preacher or organizer or community leader who would take on American exceptionalism and Manifest Destiny. The Academy Award nominated film, *Matewan* (1987), offers another labor narrative in the context of a 1920 coal miner's strike in the hills of West Virginia (based on true events).

8. In a previous book I discussed the matter of working class loyalty to the Bible and argued there for a craft approach to scripture. See my *Blue-Collar Resistance and the Politics of Jesus: Doing Ministry with Working Class Whites* (Nashville: Abingdon Press, 2006), 94–104.

The Military and Support for Our Troops

One of the strongest ingredients of cultural traditionalism is the commitment to the military and to "our troops." In fact, so pervasive is this support for our people in the armed services that the only major division is between those who support "a single-minded reliance on military force as the solution to our problems" in contrast to working people who stand for "a more cautious approach" and want military power employed "in a more limited and careful way." Meanwhile, "our men and women in uniform" received nearly constant and universal support in the major opinion polls.[9]

Let me be forthright; I come at these questions as a Christian pacifist who believes that I am "under orders" to be nonviolent, so I oppose war. At the same time, I believe that war is intrinsic to the nation-state system. I do not expect the end of war in our present geopolitical situation. I see my calling as one of urging the church in its own life to be nonviolent and of working for peace in my own country, especially to resist the elective wars that have been so much a part of US history. Such a conviction places me at odds with the great majority of white working-class people and others in the American church. So how do we deal with the question of our military?

My "approach" is to be anti-war and pro-soldier. By pro-soldier I take into account two things. First, I try to be sensitive to the relationship of working people to the military. Our military is interracial and, while virtually all of the enlisted men and women in the armed services are high school graduates, less than 3.5 percent have completed a bachelor's degree, and only 10 percent have attended college at all. The military is "one of the most homogeneously working-class institutions in America." Further, members of the military come predominately from working-class cities and towns in the heartland of America, and these troops and working-class people are bound together by common class values. Working-class people identify with these military personnel and support them with strong conviction.[10]

---

9. Andrew Levison, *The White Working Class Today: Who They Are, How They Think and How Progressives Can Regain Their Support* (Washington, DC: Democratic Strategist Press, 2013), 109–10.

10. Ibid., 158–59.

As indicated, however, there are two distinct views within the white working class about the military. One group takes "a militaristic view," holding that America has the "right to impose American values and institutions on other countries using force." The other view is more cautious and would "avoid foreign wars unless genuinely necessary for the security of the United States." These two views hold up both in the abstract and with regard to more specific wars, for example, between those who want to "stay the course to achieve stability and finish the job in Afghanistan," on the one hand, and those who believe "we need to start reducing the troops in Afghanistan," on the other hand.[11]

Second, by being pro-soldier, I want far more attention paid to the lived reality of our military personnel, especially their experiences in combat. I resent the cheap comment that says, "Thank you for your service." Such a reflex comment is typically oblivious to the hardship, and, for some, the killing in which our military members have had to engage.

In a very sensitive piece, Stanley Hauerwas discusses the sacrifices of war. He reminds us that in combat a soldier is required to sacrifice "our normal unwillingness to kill."[12] He examines a number of accounts of combat and reminds us how difficult it actually is to get soldiers to fight. A study of World War II found that of every one hundred men under enemy fire, only about fifteen to twenty would actually use their weapons.[13] In this connection, I remember a conversation I had with an instructor from the War College at Fort Leavenworth, Kansas. He told me that the most difficult thing to train a soldier to do was to fire his or her weapon in combat. He made it clear that the soldiers would not die for America, for freedom, or any other such abstraction. The only thing that "worked" was to build bonding between the soldiers and their unit. They would fight only for their buddies.

Hauerwas further addresses the difficulty of getting veterans who have killed to talk about combat. Having myself spent time with combat vets from World War II, Korea, Vietnam, Iraq, and Afghanistan, I have never found

---

11. Ibid., 159.

12. Stanley Hauerwas, *War and the American Difference: Theological Reflections on Violence and National Identity* (Grand Rapids, MI: Baker Academic, 2011), 61.

13. Ibid., 62.

one, not one, who wanted to talk about his fighting experience, and certainly not his having killed. As Hauerwas suggests, "the private nature of killing" makes such talk extremely difficult. One account reports an initial "euphoria" because the soldier survived the engagement, but then an "overwhelming guilt" for taking the life of another person. "Often this guilt is so strong that the one who has killed is wracked by physical revulsion and vomiting."[14]

My point here is that it is crucial to be pro-soldier and in a very telling way. It is not enough to *thank* our military personnel for their service. It is not enough to talk about their sacrifice and their heroism. We need far thicker descriptions[15] of what happens to our soldiers. We need far more telling accounts of how we got into wars in Vietnam, Iraq, and Afghanistan, and how the elective character of those wars placed our working-class young people so directly in harm's way. The best way to do this is through the concrete stories of how Kennedy, Johnson, the Bushes, and Obama took us into or kept us engaged in wars we did not have to choose and sent our military personnel into battles they should not have had to fight.

Further, we need to tell the stories—the flesh and blood stories—of what our soldiers have to face. Perhaps, then, their sacrifices would not be obscured by easy references to "service," "heroism," and "honor." I think of all those jingles: "Off we go into the wild blue yonder... / [Where] we live in fame or go down in flame," or "Over hill, over dale / As we hit the dusty trail," or "Anchors Aweigh, my boys," or "From the halls of Montezuma to the shores of Tripoli, we fight our country's battles on the land as on the sea."[16] We need to move from these jingles of justification to the jungles of carnage and the deserts of butchery. We do this by identification with the military personnel, not by a self-righteous blaming of them for what our nation and we do.

14. Ibid., 63. Hauerwas is working with Lt. Col. Dave Grossman, *On Killing: The Psychological Cost of Learning to Kill in War and Society* (Boston: Little, Brown and Co., 1995), 115–16.

15. See Shelly Rambo, *Resurrecting Wounds: Living in the Afterlife of Trauma* (Waco, TX: Baylor University Press, 2017) and Larry Kent Graham, *Moral Injury: Restoring Wounded Souls* (Nashville: Abingdon Press, 2017) for more on trauma theology as a frame for healing from the trauma of wars.

16. The Marines Hymn. See http://www.marineband.marines.mil/About/Library-and -Archives/The-Marines-Hymn/.

TRAUMA AND MEMORIES OF VIOLENCE

Some years ago, theologian W. Paul Jones and I were teaching a course on prophetic ministry and addressing the issue of the human condition. To give this matter gravity in terms of both finitude and death, we arranged a visit of our class to the cadaver room of a local medical school. When we entered that space, we found tanks of formaldehyde around the walls with bodies floating in them. In the center of the room were tables where the medical students did their work. On one of those tables lying face up was a human torso: head, shoulders, chest, and arms. The lower half of the body and the insides of the chest cavity had been removed.

It took weeks for me to get "distance" on that image. Every time I sat down to eat, at night when I tried to go to sleep, and in moments when my attention was focused on entirely different subjects and events, it intruded on my life.

Not long after that, I had one of those very rare conversations with a combat veteran. Finally, able to talk with someone, he told me of the day he used an automatic weapon and literally cut a Vietcong soldier in half. The ravage of a dozen bullets blew his stomach away. After five years, my soldier friend recounted, the nightmare continued to wake him up; he found himself flinching in broad daylight when that moment broke through an entire range of seemingly unrelated daily experiences. He felt dominated by the event.

At the time, I certainly did not equate my "clinical" time in the cadaver room with the horror of combat he continued to endure, but I wondered how he and thousands upon thousands of soldiers continued to deal with demonic memories that will not go away.

Free Enterprise and the American System of Government

Studies show that in the abstract white working-class Americans support the free enterprise system, and they tend to see that system in terms of a small business perspective. It is important to remember here, however, that the great majority of the white working class is made up of people who are cultural traditionalists and not free-market conservatives.

They have a strong anti-government opinion and blame government mainly for what has happened to the economy. While they radically

153

mistrust big business, they believe that it is the role of government to prevent abuse by corporate America. Moreover, they believe that the latter has too much money and power and that the distribution of wealth and income is wrong. However, they believe there is nothing ordinary people can do about it; hence there is great despair, cynicism, and fatalism in their views.[17] At the same time there is strong support for the "American system of government"; in other words, a basic commitment to "the Constitution, the Bill of Rights, and democratic elections."[18]

Yet, when asked about more concrete and specific issues, such as support for Social Security, Medicare, and Medicaid, they are far more positive, though not in a coherent or systematic way. While there is a strong core of people on the right wing of economic issues, and a strong but less numerous group on the left, it is the more moderate group of white working-class people in the middle who are not only persuadable in one direction or another but finally determine the vote when economic issues come before the public.

From a theological standpoint there are three issues to be addressed with working-class people: human nature, monopoly capitalism versus the free market, and the ongoing but now exacerbated conflict between capitalism and a democratic country.

Human Nature

I discussed earlier the problems with the free market notion of the rational economic individual who pursues self-interest in a competitive, free market. Such a view of human nature is an abstraction of the highest order, and recent studies in behavioral economics have demonstrated this for virtually anyone except those who are ideologically entrenched. Moreover, cultural traditionalism stands in direct opposition to *homo economicus*, especially as seen through a family rhetoric.

In addition, certain images within the barrel of cultural resources of working-class people can be drawn upon to make quite valid theological claims. There are those images of people who are tight-assed,

---

17. See the discussion in Levison, *The White Working Class Today*, 171–203.

18. Ibid., 86.

have tunnel-vision, are narrowly focused on self-interest, are blatantly unaware of the world around them, are unable to let their hair down, and are lacking in the ability just to have a good time. When I worked in the oil field I heard the comment made about such people: "They are so tight-assed they make love with a wet washrag in their hands," suggesting that they were so utility- and instrumentally oriented in every dimension of their lives that they could not even relax and enjoy something as extraordinarily expressive as erotic lovemaking without being at the ready for a calculated, sanitized clean up. We need precisely this kind of counterattack on the rational economic, utilitarian individualism touted by an intellectually depleted ideology. To claim that such individualism is human nature is an attempt to "naturalize" a human aberration. Indeed, breaking someone out of this kind of captivity is a liberative and salvific act.

Even more important, when this view of human nature is placed against the idea of a human being as created in the image of God, who is called to live out a life of love and justice for the other, the differences between these two images of human being are stark.

Monopoly Capitalism versus the Free Market

The second issue is to raise questions with the notion of free enterprise by means of the looming monopoly capitalism of a global economy. Working-class people know what the global economy has done to their lives, and they are not oblivious to the monopolization of markets occurring in United States and across the world. From a theological perspective these economic developments are best seen in terms of the New Testament notion of principalities and powers, the "fallen" forces that shape and determine our lives together. The point is that on matters of this kind we begin the theological work at the point of their pain, alienation, and fierce anger. The job is to name the powers and, again, to trace their impact on their lives and those of their reciprocating kin, and from there to the families of those who are other.

About free enterprise, it is also important to make the historical point that there has never been a truly free enterprise economy on earth. There have been relatively free markets; and, yes, a relatively free market can make important contributions to an economy, such as making production more efficient and determining prices. To suggest, however, that such markets can or should operate without being subject to "ruling authorities" is a strangely unbelievable argument for the very people who so often argue "law and order."

Capitalism and a Democratic Country

The third issue is the long-standing conflict between a capitalist economy and a democratic country; that is, can representative democracy survive in a global system of massive, deregulated, multinational corporations? Wolfgang Streeck argues that the conflict between capitalism and democracy has now been won by capitalism. We are no longer "one-citizen-one-vote"; we are now "one-dollar-one-vote."[19] This circumstance is understood well by white working-class people. The problem is that they blame government too exclusively, on the one hand, and are too fatalistic or pessimistic about being able to do anything about big business, on the other.

This is an important point for the sharpest kind of theological critique. The enormous imbalances in wealth and income simply cannot be defended morally or theologically, and the capacity of the rich and corporate America to buy off Congress goes against everything that the Constitution, Bill of Rights, and our system of law finally claim; not to mention that it violates the sensibilities of all of the major faith traditions of this country and of all the world.

In the afterword of Daniel Bell's classic book, *The Cultural Contradictions of Capitalism*, he reaffirms a claim from the first edition of that work that in capitalism and modernism with "their insatiable bursting of all bonds, there was 'nothing sacred.'" Bell goes on to say: "In the West, in the economic and cultural realms, the Protestant ethic (now a mythos) has been overwhelmed by acquisitiveness, and Modernism has ended in the morass of postmodernism and PoMo." Not a

---

19. Wolfgang Streeck, *How Will Capitalism End? Essays on a Failing System* (New York: Verso, 2016), 73–77.

believer himself, Bell explains that what he means by the sacred is "not the sphere of God or of the gods." It is, however, an indispensable one, "of what is beyond us and cannot be transgressed."[20] I agree, but on theological grounds.

The dominating power of a rapacious capitalism that has subverted this democratic republic is a charge that white working-class people can hear. Theological criticism based in scripture has authoritative power. I think of Isaiah 5:8:

> Doom to those who acquire house after house,
> who annex field to field until there is no more space left
> and only you live alone in the land.

There is a powerful text in Ezekiel where the word of the Lord speaks through the prophet about the conspiracy of princes, the unholiness of priests, the corruption of officials, the false testimony of prophets, and the violations of important people, who "have practiced extortion and have committed robbery. They've oppressed the poor and mistreated the immigrant. They've oppressed and denied justice" (22:29). But the biblical testimony is immense. For only a few examples, see Job 29:11-17; 31:13-23; Amos 5:21-24; Luke 4:16-21.

Here is where it is important not only to think theology but to do theology. In the previous chapter we suggested a number of ways that white working-class people in coalition with others can take action on issues that radically affect their lives. Two things, for example, can be taken on by local groups in coalition. The first of these is to remove the huge contributions to political campaigns. This needs to be done at both the state and the national levels. The second thing is to move from partisan gerrymandering to a more neutral designing of electoral districts. This kind of doing theology is necessary to address the powers we confront.

---

20. Daniel Bell, *The Cultural Contradictions of Capitalism: Twentieth Anniversary Edition* (New York: Basic Books, 1996), 388.

The Common Good versus the Progressive Agenda

It is time to bring these challenging discussions to a close. By now, I hope it is clear where I stand on the great issues of our day and on my support for white working-class Americans. I want that to be clear because of where I go next and finally to conclude my remarks. For a good many years I described myself as a liberal, but the more I realized how much that term was wrapped up with certain views of the nation-state, and too accommodated to certain positions within capitalism, the more the term no longer fit. When many of my friends became "progressives," I never could quite accept the name; and, quite frankly, it had an elitist ring about it that gave me discomfort. It carried the connotation of being literate, highly educated, and professional. I am *all* of those things, I suppose, but the term felt to me as though it left out a whole bunch of people. Many of my friends who are people of color do not describe themselves that way, and even more of my white working-class friends would not be caught dead using the term. I have not used it to describe myself for some time.

Increasingly the term that speaks to me is that of the *common good* to describe the aim or end that I seek in both my academic study and my community work. It is a notion that is found in inchoate form in scripture. I think, for example, of the book of Jeremiah where God instructs the people of Israel to "promote the welfare of the city where I have sent you into exile. Pray to the Lord for it, because your future depends on its welfare" (29:7). Jeremiah is speaking to people who have been taken from Jerusalem to Babylon, from the center of their ancestral life to be exiles and strangers in the capital city of their captors. Yet God, through Jeremiah, tells these Israelites to seek the welfare of that city because their welfare depends upon that of Babylon.

I also think of the apostle Paul and the fact that in every one of his authentic letters he urges the people of the *ecclesia* he organized to seek the good of all. It is a persistent theme in his work. I am also aware of the ways that Jesus crossed lines continually to heal, teach, and make alive.

The notion of the common good also reaches back into the rich tradition of the church in thinkers like Augustine, Thomas, Luther, Calvin, and in contemporary Catholic and Protestant thought. Further, I have found it to be very important in interfaith work, where I have been seriously engaged.

One clarification seems to be desperately important: we do not know ahead of time what the common good is. I find it to be a decidedly grassroots, bottom-up process. Abstract notions such as social justice, distributive justice, democratic participation, and so on, require a very concrete embodiment in the lives and group processes of down on the ground, real life people. I am especially suspicious of progressive agendas developed by elites who then go out and attempt to organize and mobilize people on their behalf. I find it especially problematic to attempt this with white working-class people. It should also be obvious that I detest the use of high-sounding language to promote the unjustified and viciously self-interested aims of right-wing billionaires and their gigolo congressional leaders as in the so-called tax reduction bill of December, 2017.

The common good is a discovery, a find. It emerges from a process of listening, conversation, and building relationships and trust. It is local without being parochial. It is more than individual or group interest, taken alone. It grows out of what people truly need and profoundly love. It requires the search for common ground, a coming together that makes possible a commitment to the common good. My friend Sam Mann says that moving toward, moving onto a common ground is an act of love. In community organizing it is a moment that becomes a relationship—one that generates a commitment—a commitment that enters people of differences onto a journey. The character of that journey is not "all glory hallelujah mountain time" (a time of high emotional expression and joy); rather it becomes the discipline of showing up, being there, staying the course, and being willing to act. It's doing the scut work of detail and follow-up, making phone calls, and touching base. It is opening up to one who is other. It is a response to the pain of others but also to their hopes and dreams. It's sorting out the pieces of life: putting them together in new configurations and working those compositions into the common good. This may sound lofty, but it is hard work; it's digging on hardscrabble ground. It's staying with it long after you want to quit.[21] In a Christian understanding it is born not of optimism but of hope and a confidence that God bats last.

---

21. I am indebted to Stanley Hauerwas for his understanding of the common good as a discovery. See his *Vision and Virtue: Essays in Christian Ethical Reflection* (Notre Dame, IN: Notre Dame Press, 1981), 235–40; and his more recent *War and the American Difference: Theological Reflections on Violence and National Identity* (Ada, MI: Baker Academic, 2011), 140–50. For the notion of the common good as local but not parochial, see Charles M. Payne, *I've Got the Light of Freedom: The Organizing Tradition and the Mississippi Freedom Struggle* (Berkeley: University of California Press, 1995), 101. I am also indebted to my friend Sam Mann for a stimulating conversation about common ground on December 6, 2017. Sam said more than I have room to write, but I am truly grateful for his help.

AFTERWORD

We have named a number of the difficulties that confront white working-class Americans in the basic context of their lives. These are systemic and structural contributors to a deep and pervasive anger. In attempting to identify these white working-class people, we have reported important statistical data and key attempts to define who they are. While useful, these are not adequate to the complexity of this important group of Americans. We provided summaries of six ethnographic studies of working people in urban and rural America. We then examined racism in both its prejudicial and systemic and structural forms in order to not only challenge the scapegoating of white working-class people on this issue but also to diagnose more carefully its various forms—especially among white working-class people—in order to be able to take more effective action. We next moved to a chapter on the more micro, granular, indigenous practices of white working-class people so that we knew how to move not just more effectively but also with more respect for their idioms and practices. As important as this indigenous work is, we must also move into grassroots, down on the ground community action, which we did by reporting work being done in cities and counties in urban and rural America by means of single-issue and coalition strategies and through city and state referenda. This approach convinces me that the situation of white working-class Americans and working-class people of color is not hopeless; but, instead, is an opportune time for significant social change. We then provided biblical and theological rationale by which, on the one hand, to critique white working-class commitments; but, on the other hand, to affirm central dimensions of their culture that open doors economically, politically, and spiritually for more faithful and vital life. May it be so.

BIBLIOGRAPHY

Abramowitz, Alan, and Roy Texeira. "The Decline of the White Working Class and the Rise of a Mass Upper-Middle Class." Brookings Institute. April 8, 2008. https://www.brookings.edu/research/the-decline-of-the-white-working-class-and-the-rise-of-a-mass-upper-middle-class/.

Alcoff, Linda Martín. *The Future of Whiteness*. Malden, MA: Polity Press, 2015.

Alexander, Michelle. *The New Jim Crow: Mass Incarceration in the Age of Colorblindness*. New York: The New Press, 2012.

Allport, Gordon W. *The Nature of Prejudice*. Reading, MA: Addison-Wesley, 1954.

Asad, Talal. *Genealogies of Religion*. Baltimore: Johns Hopkins University Press, 2009.

Ault, James M. Jr. *Spirit and Flesh: Life in a Fundamentalist Baptist Church*. New York: Knopf, 2004.

Bageant, Joe. *Deer Hunting with Jesus: Dispatches from America's Class War*. New York: Crown Publishers, 2007.

Barber, Benjamin. "In the Age of Donald Trump, the Resistance Will Be Localized." *The Nation*, January 18, 2017. https://www.thenation.com/article/in-the-age-of-donald-trump-the-resistance-will-be-localized/.

Barber, The Rev. Dr. William J. II, with Jonathan Wilson-Hartgrove. *The Third Reconstruction: Moral Mondays, Fusion Politics, and the Rise of a New Justice Movement*. Boston: Beacon Press, 2016.

Bell, Daniel. *The Cultural Contradictions of Capitalism*. Twentieth Anniversary Edition. New York: Basic Books, 1996.

Bivens, Josh, and Lawrence Mishel. "Understanding the Historic Divergence between Productivity and a Typical Worker's Pay: Why It Matters and Why It's Real." Briefing Paper 406. Economic Policy Institute. September 2, 2015. https://www.epi.org/publication/understanding-the-historic-divergence-between-productivity-and-a-typical-workers-pay-why-it-matters-and-why-its-real/.

Blount, Brian K. *Revelation: A Commentary.* The New Testament Library. Louisville, KY: Westminster John Knox Press, 2009.

Carnes, Nicholas and Noam Lupu. "It's Time to Bust the Myth: Most Trump Voters Were Not Working Class." *The Washington Post,* June 5, 2017. https://www.washingtonpost.com/news/monkey-cage/wp/2017/06/05/its-time-to-bust-the-myth-most-trump-voters-were-not-working-class/?utm_term=.7166075682c6.

Cash, W. J. *The Mind of the South* (New York: Vintage Books, 1991).

Chetty, Raj, and David Grusky, Maximilian Hell, Nathaniel Hendren, Robert Manduca, and Jimmy Narang. "The Fading American Dream: Trends in Absolute Income Mobility since 1940." *Science*, April 24, 2017. http://science.sciencemag.org/content/early/2017/04/21/science.aal4617.full.

Clean Missouri Initiative. www.cleanmissouri.org/soloution/.

Congress.gov. Amendments to the Constitution of the United States of America. https://www.congress.gov/content/conan/pdf/GPO-CONAN-2017-7.pdf.

Cramer, Katherine. *The Politics of Resentment: Rural Consciousness in Wisconsin and the Rise of Scott Walker.* Chicago: University of Chicago Press, 2016.

Cummings, Ian, "Walmart's Bleeding This Town, Raytown Official Says." *The Kansas City Star*, September 28, 2017, 6A.

Du Bois, W. E. B. *Black Reconstruction in America: An Essay toward a History of the Part Which Black Folk Played in the Attempt to Reconstruct Democracy in America, 1860–1880.* New York: Free Press, 1997.

Edsall, Thomas B. "The 2016 Exit Polls Led Us to Misinterpret the 2016 Election." The New York Times, March 29, 2018. https://www.nytimes.com/2018/03/29/opinion/2016-exit-polls-election.html.

Ehrenfreund, Max and Jeff Guo. "If You've Ever Described People as 'White Working Class,' Read This." *The Washington Post*, November 23, 2016. https://

www.washingtonpost.com/news/wonk/wp/2016/11/22/who-exactly-is
-the-white-working-class-and-what-do-they-believe-good-questions/?utm
_term=.5a495aca2bc2.

Ehrenreich, Barbara, "Dead, White, and Blue." *Guernica*, December 1, 2015. https://
www.guernicamag.com/barbara-ehrenreich-dead-white-and-blue/.

_____. *Nickel and Dimed*. New York: Owl Books, 2002.

Fox, Aaron A. *Real Country: Music and Language in Working-Class Culture*. Durham,
NC: Duke University Press, 2004.

Frank, Thomas. *Listen Liberal; or, Whatever Happened to the Party of the People*. New
York: Metropolitan Books, 2016.

_____. *What's the Matter with Kansas? How Conservatives Won the Heart of America*.
New York: Owl Books, 2005.

Gest, Justin. *The New Minority: White Working Class Politics in an Age of Immigration
and Inequality*. New York: Oxford University Press, 2016.

Giddens, Anthony. *Central Problems in Social Theory: Action, Structure, and Contradiction in Social Theory*. Berkeley: University of California Press, 1979.

Gilens, Martin and Benjamin I. Page, "Testing Theories of American Politics: Elites,
Interest Groups, and Average Citizens." *Perspectives on Politics* 12, no. 3 (September 2014): 564–81, accessed December 8, 2017, https://scholar.princ
eton.edu/sites/default/files/mgilens/files/gilens_and_page_2014_-testing
_theories_of_american_politics.doc.pdf.

Gould, Skye, and Rebecca Harrington. "7 Charts Show Who Propelled Trump to
Victory." Edison Research for the National Pool. *Business Insider*, November
10, 2016.

Graham, Larry Kent. *Moral Injury: Restoring Wounded Souls*. Nashville: Abingdon
Press, 2017.

Grossman, Lt. Col. Dave. *On Killing: The Psychological Cost of Learning to Kill in War
and Society*. Boston: Little, Brown and Co., 1995.

Harink, Douglas. *Paul among the Postliberals: Pauline Theology beyond Christendom
and Modernity*. Grand Rapids, MI: Brazos Press, 2003.

Hauerwas, Stanley. *Vision and Virtue: Essays in Christian Ethical Reflection.* Notre Dame, IN: Notre Dame Press, 1981, 235–40.

_____. *War and the American Difference: Theological Reflections on Violence and National Identity.* Grand Rapids, MI: Baker Academic, 2011.

Hightower, Jim. "You'll Be Gobsmacked by the Populist Victories Won in This Conservative Colorado Town." *The Hightower Lowdown,* July 19, 2017. https://hightowerlowdown.org/article/colorado-springs/.

Hirschkind, Charles and David Scott, eds. *Powers of the Secular Modern: Talal Asad and His Interlocutors.* Stanford, CA: Stanford University Press.

Hochschild, Arlie Russell. *Strangers in Their Own Land: Anger and Mourning on the American Right.* New York: The New Press, 2016.

Howell, Joseph T. *Hard Living on Clay Street: Portraits of Blue-Collar Families.* New York: Anchor Books, 1973.

Isenberg, Nancy. *White Trash: The 400-Year History of Class in America.* New York: Viking, 2016.

Johnston, David Cay. *Free Lunch: How the Wealthiest Americans Enrich Themselves at Government Expense and Stick You with the Bill.* New York: Penguin Books, 2007.

Jones, Robert P., and Daniel Cox. "Beyond Guns and God: Understanding the Complexity of the White Working Class in America." Public Religion Research Institute, February 20, 2012. https://www.prri.org/research/race-class-culture-survey-2012/.

Kansas City Star, The. "To Get a Crime-Ridden Walmart, Raytown Gave Away the Store." Editorials. September 29, 2017, 12A.

Kee, Howard Clark, Emily Albu Hanawalt, Carter Lindberg, Jean Loup Seban, and Mark A. Knoll. Epilogue by Dana L. Robert. *Christianity: A Social and Cultural History.* New York: Macmillan, 1991.

Kumkar, Nils. "A Socio-Analysis of Discontent: Protest against the Politics of Crisis in the U.S. and Germany: An Empirical Comparison." PhD thesis, University of Leipzig, 2015.

Lakoff, George. *Don't Think of an Elephant! Know Your Values and Frame the Debate—*

The Essential Guide for Progressives. White River Junction, VT: Chelsea Green Publishers, 2004.

_____. *Moral Politics: How Liberals and Conservatives Think*. 2nd ed. Chicago: University of Chicago Press, 2002.

Lamont, Michèle. *The Dignity of Working Men: Morality and the Boundaries of Race, Class, and Immigration*. Cambridge, MA: Harvard University Press, 2000.

Lamont, Michèle and Marcel Fournier, eds. *Cultivating Differences: Symbolic Boundaries and the Making of Inequality*. Chicago: University of Chicago Press, 1992.

Leonhardt, David. "The American Dream, Quantified at Last." Sunday Review. *New York Times*, December 8, 2016. https://www.nytimes.com/2016/12/08/opinion/the-american-dream-quantified-at-last.html.

Levison, Andrew. "Is There a Viable Progressive Strategy to Increase White Working Class Support in the 'Conservative Heartland'?" *The Democratic Strategist*, 2017. http://thedemocraticstrategist-roundtables.com/is-there-a-viable-progressive-strategy-to-increase-white-working-class-support-in-the-conservative-heartland/.

_____. *The White Working Class Today: Who They Are, How They Think and How Progressives Can Regain Their Support*. Washington, DC: Democratic Strategist Press, 2013.

MacIntyre, Alasdair. *After Virtue: A Study in Moral Theory*. 2nd edition. Notre Dame, IN: Notre Dame Press, 1984.

McDermott, Monica. *Working-Class White: The Making and Unmaking of Race Relations*. Berkeley: University of California Press, 2006.

Missouri Rural Crisis Center. "CAFO Threatens Howard County." 2016.

Oxfam Media Briefing, "Broken at the Top." Oxfam America, April 14, 2016, https://www.oxfamamerica.org/static/media/files/Broken_at_the_Top_4.14.2016.pdf.

Payne, Charles M. *I've Got the Light of Freedom: The Organizing Tradition and the Mississippi Freedom Struggle*. Berkeley: University of California Press, 1995.

Pew Research Center. "Changing Composition of the Electorate and Partisan Coalitions." In Wide Gender Gap, Growing Educational Divide in Voters'

Party Identification. http://assets.pewresearch.org/wp-content/uploads/sites /5/2018/03/20113922/03-20-18-Party-Identification.pdf.

Pilkington, John. "Obama Angers Midwest Voters with Guns and Religion Remark." *The Guardian*, April 14, 2008. https://www.theguardian.com/world/2008 /apr/14/barackobama.uselections2008.

Preheim, Rich. "Report Reveals Full History of Theologian's Abuse, Institutions' Response." *The Christian Century*, February 17, 2015.

Putnam, Robert D., Carl B. Frederick, and Kaisa Snellman. "Growing Class Gaps in Social Connectedness among American Youth." *The Saguaro Seminar: Civic Engagement in America*. Cambridge, MA: Harvard Kennedy School of Government, 2012.

Reilly, Katie. "Read Hillary Clinton's 'Basket of Deplorables' Remarks about Donald Trump Supporters." Time on Scene, September 10, 2016. http://time .com/4486502/hillary-clinton-basket-of-deplorables-transcript/.

Richard, Pablo. *Apocalypse: A People's Commentary on the Book of Revelation*. Mary knoll, NY: Orbis Books, 1995.

Rambo, Shelly. *Resurrecting Wounds: Living in the Afterlife of Trauma*. Waco, TX: Baylor University Press, 2017.

Roediger, David R. *The Wages of Whiteness: Race and the Making of the American Working Class*. Rev. ed. New York: Verso, 1999.

Rothstein, Richard. "The Making of Ferguson: Executive Summary." Economic Policy Institute, October 15, 2014. http://www.epi.org/publication/making -ferguson/.

Royce, Edward. *Poverty and Power: The Problem of Structural Inequality*. New York: Rowman and Littlefield, 2009.

Sahadi, Jeanne. "The Richest 10% Hold 76% of the Wealth." CNN Money, August 18, 2016. http://money.cnn.com/2016/08/18/pf/wealth-inequality/index.html.

Sample, Tex. *Blue Collar Ministry: Facing Economic and Social Realities of Working People*. Valley Forge, PA: Judson Press, 1984.

_____. *Blue Collar Resistance and the Politics of Jesus: Doing Ministry with Working Class Whites*. Nashville: Abingdon Press, 2006.

_____. *Hard Living People and Mainstream Christians*. Nashville: Abingdon Press, 1993.

_____. "Laughing at What I Love: Notes on White Working-Class America." *Reflections*. Yale University Divinity School, 2013.

_____. *Ministry in an Oral Culture: Living with Will Rogers, Uncle Remus, and Minnie Pearl*. Louisville, KY: Westminster John Knox Press, 1994.

Sherman, Jennifer. *Those Who Work, Those Who Don't: Poverty, Morality, and Family in Rural America*. Minneapolis: University of Minnesota Press, 2009.

Shipler, David K. *The Working Poor: Invisible in America*. New York: Vintage, 2005.

Skocpol, Theda, and Vanessa Williams. *The Tea Party and the Remaking of Republican Conservatism*. New York: Oxford University Press, 2012.

Smith, Dina. "Cultural Studies' Misfit: White Trash Studies." *Mississippi Quarterly* LVII, no. 3 (Summer 2004).

Stiglitz, Joseph. *Globalization and Its Discontents*. New York: W. W. Norton, 2002.

_____. "There Is No Invisible Hand." *The Guardian*, December 20, 2002. https://www.theguardian.com/education/2002/dec/20/highereducation.uk1.

Streeck, Wolfgang. *How Will Capitalism End? Essays on a Failing System*. New York: Verso, 2016.

Vance, J. D. *Hillbilly Elegy*. New York: HarperCollins, 2016.

Wallis, Jim. *God's Politics*. New York: HarperOne, 2005.

Warren, Elizabeth. *This Fight Is Our Fight: The Battle to Save America's Middle Class*. New York: Metropolitan Books, 2017.

Wilkey, Joshua. "My Mother Wasn't Trash." The Appalachian Life blog, May 10, 2017. https://www.thisappalachialife.com/single-post/2017/05/10/My-Mother-Wasnt-Trash.

Williams, Richard. "The Dignity of Working Men and Black Identities." *Sociological Forum*, 17, no 2 (June 2002).

Woodard, Colin. *American Nations: A History of the Eleven Rival Regional Cultures of North America*. New York: Penguin Books, 2011.

Wright, Erik Olin. *Understanding Class*. New York: Verso, 2015.

Yoder, John Howard. "On Not Being Ashamed of the Gospel." *Faith and Philosophy* 9 (1992).

_____. *The Politics of Jesus: Vicit Agnus Noster*. Grand Rapids, MI: William B. Eerdmans, 1972.

_____. *The Priestly Kingdom: Social Ethics as Gospel*. Notre Dame: Notre Dame Press, 1984.

Zinn, Howard. *A People's History of the United States*. New York: Harper and Row, 1980.